ANDY WIGHTMAN is a graduate in forestry from Aberdeen University and has worked as a forestry contractor, woodcutter, stalker's ghillie, land-use scientist and environmental campaigner, and is now a freelance writer, researcher and analyst specialising in land tenure & ownership, land reform and rural development. The author of *Who Owns Scotland* (Canongate Books, 1996), he has written a wide range of reports and articles on land-related topics and is a leading advocate of land reform in Scotland. He acts as an advisor to a number of organisations and individuals both private and public and is currently engaged in analysis and research on various aspects of land reform.

DEMOCRATIC LEFT SCOTLAND is a campaigning network working towards a fairer and more equal society. Democracy and equality are the core values shared by its members, who are active in many diverse movements and campaigns.

Democratic Left Scotland believes in the importance of ideas, discussion and debate to empower people to participate in politics.

As a signatory to the Claim of Right and a member of the Scottish Constitutional Convention prior to the establishment of Scotland's Parliament, Democratic Left Scotland continues to uphold the principle of the sovereignty of the Scottish people in its work.

D0278026

Show the people that our
Old Nobility is not noble,
that its lands are stolen lands –
stolen either by force or fraud;
show people that the title-deeds
are rapine, murder, massacre,
cheating, or Court harlotry;
dissolve the halo of divinity that
surrounds the hereditary title;
let the people clearly
understand that our present
House of Lords is composed
largely of descendants of
successful pirates and rogues;
do these things and you shatter
the Romance that keeps the
nation numb and spellbound
while privilege picks its pocket.

Tom Johnston, Secretary of State for Scotland
from *Our Scots Noble Families* 1909 (reprinted 1999,
Argyll Publishing)

Scotland:
Land and Power
The Agenda for Land Reform

ANDY WIGHTMAN

Luath Press Limited
EDINBURGH
www.luath.co.uk

AUTHOR'S ACKNOWLEDGEMENTS

I wish to thank Democratic Left Scotland for asking me to
write what has turned out to be a small book, but which
started life as a modest political pamphlet. It was perceptive
and far-sighted of them to choose the topic of land and power
in Scotland for analysis and enquiry at a time of unparalleled
political interest. Thanks in particular to Douglas Chalmers,
Seb Fischer, Susan Moffat, and Eurig Scandrett for their
patience and commitment to the project.

Robin Callander and Graham Boyd have also provided much-
needed help and support along the way, for which I am
extremely grateful.

Finally, I want to pay tribute to all those people who, over the
years, and in a hostile political environment, have kept the
land reform agenda alive and inspired my own activity. Don't
disappear now!

First Edition 1999
Reprinted 2000

The paper used in this book is recyclable. It is made from low
chlorine pulps produced in a low energy, low emission manner
from renewable forests.

Printed and bound by
Omnia Books Ltd., Glasgow

Illustrations by Terry Anderson, Scottish Cartoon Art Studio,
Glasgow; captions by Andy Wightman

Edited by Jennie Renton

Design by Tom Bee

Typeset in 10.5 point Sabon by
S. Fairgrieve, Edinburgh

© Andy Wightman

Contents

Preface		7
Foreword		9
Introduction		11

CHAPTER 1	First a Bit of History	15
	The Patronage of the Monarch	16
	Revolution	21
	The 20th Century	23

CHAPTER 2	Scotland – A Feudal Land at the Onset of a New Millenium	27
	The End of Feudalism	29
	The Pattern of Landownership	30
	Landed Hegemony	31
	Property Law	35
	Politics	36
	Wealth	37
	Inheritance	38
	Tax	39
	The Unregulated Market	40
	Conclusions	41

CHAPTER 3	So What is Land Reform?	43
	What is Land?	44
	The Economic Discourse	45
	The Political Discourse	47
	The Environmental Discourse	48
	Theology	49
	Land Reform in Scotland Today	50

CHAPTER 4	The Politics of Land Reform	53
	The Landed Interest	57
	A Radical Agenda	62
	The Highlandification of Land Reform	65

CHAPTER 5 A Critique of Existing Proposals   68
           The Abolition of Feudalism   68
           The Fashionable Idea of
           Community   72
           Community Ownership   73
           Community Involvement   79
           Room for Hope   81

CHAPTER 6 A Land Reform Programme   83
           1. Tenure   86
           2. Land Values   87
           3. Information   89
           4. Holding Size   90
           5. Tenant Right-to-Buy   92
           6. Residency   94
           7. Succession Law Reform   95
           8. Offshore Trusts & Companies
               and Private Trusts   97
           9. The Land Market   99
           10. The Urban Agenda   101
           A Wider Land Reform Agenda   102
           So Will This Happen?   103

CHAPTER 7 Ah But!   105

CHAPTER 8 Conclusions   113
           New Opportunities?   113
           Political Realities   115

Explanatory Notes   120
Some Further Reading   125

Preface

For too long the debate on land reform has remained marginalised and concentrated in the hands and minds of too few people. Yet most people in Scotland share strong unease and intuitive opposition to the concentration of power in the hands of a privileged few. We believe the issue of land reform deserves a broader and more embracing public debate so that all the arguments can be scrutinised by many more people.

The political discourse around land ownership has, by and large, been a safe debate. Nobody, it appears, wants to offend – least of all offend those who currently benefit most from unaccountable inherited wealth and privilege. It feels as if all the main political parties are conniving in a cosy consensus, proclaiming 'radical' change while avoiding any fundamental challenge to the vested political and economic power of the land-owning elite in Scotland.

In political, economic and social terms, ownership and power over land remain decisive factors of social exclusion. Land reform could potentially reverse the depopulation of vast areas of Scotland and transform economic trends, poverty and homelessness – just a few of the good reasons why a more informed debate is desirable. Of course, one publication does not bring about radical renewal, but it will help to broaden the debate. We are grateful to Andy Wightman and Luath Press for allowing this book to be produced at an affordable price. It will give many more people access to the real debate.

Land reform will be an important yardstick by which to measure real democratic change. Whether the new Scotland is indeed the dawn of a new era of democracy can be judged by how long it will take for the ideas and proposals in this book to come to fruition.

Members of Democratic Left Scotland have a vision of a society free from inequalities. Our aim is to challenge the imbalance of power created by the control of society's wealth by a minority of institutions and individuals. We argue for the expansion of democratic public participation and control and advocate economic and social strategies based on democratic

planning. We therefore think there is a strong case for
fundamental, far-reaching and radical land reform for the new
millennium.

We hope readers will agree and take up these issues in their
local communities, at work and with politicians locally and in
the Scottish Parliament.

Morag Parnell
Democratic Left Scotland

Foreword

To the innocent bystander the pressure for land reform in Scotland seems to have come from nowhere. The fact that a rural and legal sounding issue has managed to penetrate the ignorance and apathy of Britain's urban political elite is partly due to the ground breaking buy-outs of Assynt and Eigg and partly due to the efforts of people like Andy Wightman.

The first man to catalogue the overwhelming scale of private landownership in Scotland was the forester John McEwen whose book *Who Owns Scotland* so shocked Scottish civic society in the 1970s. At around the same time the 7:84 Theatre Company was touring its first major play, *The Cheviot, the Stag and the Black, Black Oil*. It laid bare some of the unwritten and unspoken rules of Highland society and for the first time many locals saw the power of the Laird ridiculed and parodied in public. Jaws dropped. But the old ways went on.

It took John McEwen years to chronicle who owns what in Scotland. And within months of publication his painstaking snapshot of land ownership inevitably became inaccurate. Decades later Andy Wightman valiantly revisited the task and after an epic voyage of discovery – occasionally busking his way into the front rooms of estate lodges to note down land boundaries from secret maps and pictures – he produced *Who Owns Scotland*. It revealed that a tiny number of individuals and companies controlled a sizeable chunk of Scotland with public bodies like the Forestry Commission often behaving just as high-handedly as the worst individual absentee landowner.

The refusal to cash in on tabloid caricatures and stereotypes is a key feature of all Andy's work. This book's critique of 'The Fashionable Idea of Community' may come as a surprise to those who know about his involvement with the people of Eigg whose buyout of the Hebridean island in 1997 put land reform back on the political map. Activists and local politicians backed the campaign and public appeal which eventually raised over one and a half million pounds to buy the island on the open market from its eccentric German owner, the mysterious fire artist known as Maruma. Many MPs and national politicians were conspicuous by their absence from the early years of that campaign – until it was clear that tenacity and courage had paid off and a historic buyout was in the offing.

Not surprisingly then the aim for legislation in the new
Scottish parliament has been to produce a system of land
reform that is Eigg-proof. But as Andy makes clear – that is
attractive but not good enough.

Should rural Scots have to make the substantial act of faith
and organisation that's required to make a community bid,
simply to have access to a couple of acres of land? Why
should individual tenant farmers not be given the right to buy
their land? If one or two city dwellers want to extend their
house or site a workshop or even build a few houses they
aren't exhorted to work with the rest of the street to make a
community business venture out of their idea first. Why
should rural Scots be different?

Are they more co-operative people? Not necessarily. The only
reason many will even consider a community buy-out of their
land is that no other solution is on offer.

And one suspects that's because the social and political
objective upon which politicians are agreed is simply to make
sure nothing as embarrassing as Eigg ever happens again.
Andy Wightman is arguing for something more far reaching
and radical – that supporting people to stay on the land is a
good thing, that giving them control of local assets is an
economically sensible thing, that breaking up large estates and
thereby lowering land values is an essential thing and that
living amongst purposeful, empowered and active
communities of Scots might be a very exciting thing.

This book will therefore not make easy reading for those who
think that land can be dealt with by a few quick fixes. Scotland's
rural communities have been scarred by a wilful ignorance of the
damage created by the most concentrated system of
landownership in the western world. Writers like Andy
Wightman are determined to make sure the hurt of the last
century is not compounded by a rushed solution in the next.

This accessible, comprehensive, but passionately argued book
is quite simply essential reading, and perfectly timed – here's
hoping Scotland's legislators agree.

Lesley Riddoch

Introduction

After decades of being neglected and marginalised by the political process, land reform is now firmly on the political agenda. The election of the Labour Government in May 1997 and the establishment of the Scottish Parliament have provided an opportunity to ensure that this topic can enjoy the same kind of scrutiny, analysis, debate, and action as other areas of public policy such as health, education, law and order, transport and the environment.

The Scottish Parliament removes two of the key barriers to achieving land reform. The first is the lack of time in a crowded Westminster agenda. The second barrier has been more substantial and of longer standing. The House of Lords has blocked and frustrated any proposals which threaten or appear to threaten the vested interests of its many landowning members. Neither the House of Lords nor its successor body will have a role in the scrutiny, amendment, or enactment of any legislation emanating from the Scottish Parliament. In the words of one Labour MP, Scots lairds will have to take their place in the lobby corridors along with everyone else. But the removal of these barriers and the establishment of a Scottish Parliament will not automatically deliver land reform. The political will, based on a fundamental analysis of the issue is also vital. To date, Government and opposition proposals for land reform, whilst of some utility, are based largely on flawed analyses, shallow, short-term politics, timidity and poverty of imagination.

To date, Government and opposition proposals for land reform, whilst of some utility, are based largely on flawed analyses, shallow, short-term politics, timidity and poverty of imagination.

That is not, however, wholly the fault of politicians. Because of the long neglect and wilful suppression of debate about land reform, poorly informed debate has often characterised discussions about the issue – a debate which has not been helped by the frequent media attention given to the more colourful and bizarre stories about rogue Dutchmen, offshore companies and eccentric lairds. The politics of envy and outrage, whilst providing some lively entertainment, have not succeeded in overcoming any of the deep-rooted problems that exist.

The media interest in the goings on in small, isolated (often crofting) communities in the far north and west has also tended to suggest that land reform is an issue relevant only to the more far flung parts of the country. Land reform has typically been portrayed as a rural issue, a Highland issue and an issue about bad landowners.

This book argues the case for a more fundamental and honest political approach to land reform and for a genuinely radical (i.e. going to the roots) political agenda for land reform. This agenda lies at the heart of this book and is presented in Chapter 6. It represents a programme of action which is true to the spirit of land reform, which is practical, and which draws on the essence of the European land reform tradition.

Before that, the book explores the historical background to the land question before going on to describe the current situation, thus making the connection between the past and the present. It then steps back a bit to explore what land reform actually means before moving on to look at the politics of the topic and to critique current government proposals, in particular, the fashionable idea of 'community'.

The arguments and issues presented here are unashamedly political in tone. Too frequently land reformers have been accused of pursuing a political agenda on land reform, as if there is such a thing as land reform which is not political. There is not. Land represents power and is therefore political. Trying to pretend that it isn't leads to the kind of technical and managerialist agenda that has been developed by the main Scottish political parties.

That said, land reform can equally well be viewed as an eminently pragmatic and rational response to the need to update and modernise the way in which land is owned in Scotland. Many of the measures outlined in Chapter 6 of this book are already reflected in other areas of land law (it is illegal for agricultural and crofting tenants, for example, not to reside on or close to their holdings, so why not landowners?) and have close parallels in the arrangements found in other European countries such as Ireland, Germany, Denmark and Norway.

At the heart of land reform then is the challenge of modernising and updating our land laws, redistributing power over how land is owned and used, and developing a new balance between the public and private interest in land. This book concentrates on these aspects of public policy – what might be termed the core of land reform – and does not stray into the wider field of land policy (the range of policies developed to govern and support how land is used and managed).

To begin with we have to ask why Scotland is the last country in the developed world to have a feudal system of tenure and why it has the most concentrated pattern of private landownership anywhere in Europe – first then, a bit of history.

A democracy ignorant of the past is not qualified either
to analyse the present or to shape the future.

Chapter 1
First a Bit of History

*Men make their own history, but they do not make it just
as they please; they do not make it under circumstances
chosen by themselves, but under circumstances directly
encountered, given and transmitted from the past.*

KARL MARX[1]

*A democracy ignorant of the past is not qualified either
to analyse the present or to shape the future.*

TOM JOHNSTON[2]

*The Government's approach to land reform is to focus
on the future, not the past.*

LORD SEWEL[3]

Current arrangements for the ownership, occupancy and
use of land are a product of centuries of feudalism and
landed power. The present system and pattern of
landownership are not a historical
accident, and thus to begin to
understand the problems of the present
we need to understand how the system
has evolved. An analysis of the land
question which does not focus at least
initially on the past is in no position
either to understand the present or to
make sensible changes for the future.

**The present system
and pattern of
landownership are
not a historical
accident, and thus
to begin to
understand the
problems of the
present we need to
understand how the
system has evolved.**

Scotland's history is, to a large degree, a
history of landed power. Until the 19th
century landed power was synonymous
with political power. Not surprisingly,
therefore, Scotland's system of land
tenure has protected and supported the political,
commercial and social ambitions of the ruling classes. In
1814 Sir John Sinclair, the Caithness improver and
author of the *First Statistical Account of Scotland,* was
moved to observe that 'In no country in Europe are the
rights of proprietors so well defined and so carefully

protected'.⁴ And it has been this careful definition and assiduous protection which has denied Scotland the kinds of reforms enjoyed by our west European neighbours. It all began in the 11th century with feudalism, a system of land tenure still with us today, 900 years later – an indication if ever it was needed of the resilience of Scotland's land laws and our historic failure, indeed inability, to do anything fundamental about reforming them.

The Patronage of the Monarch

The origins of the current system and pattern of landownership lie deep in Scotland's history.⁶ Feudalism, a system of governance initiated by David 1 (1084–1153), was based on the contractual relationship between the Crown and the nobility whereby powerful, loyal nobles were granted feudal charters over extensive estates in return for political, military and financial support.

At this early stage feudal charters did not confer ownership of land in the sense of that term today. What was being offered to the favoured few was the job of governing Scotland. It was a system of patronage. As time passed, however, the system gave vassals of the Crown more and more security. What started as a system of political power evolved steadily into a system of landed power, within which the aristocracy distanced themselves from financial and military obligations to the Crown and became full-blown landowners. And since the feudal system gave wide-ranging powers to the 'Great Landowners', those in possession of feudal charters manipulated and developed the system to their own advantage in order to retain as much power as possible over their land, even when it was 'feud' to others. These 'Great Landowners' became the cohesive strata – 'the landed property fraction of the bourgeoisie'⁷ – in Scottish society and later in UK society.

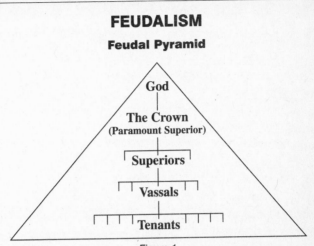

FEUDALISM

Feudal Pyramid

Figure 1

Landownership is a property system embracing the whole of Scotland from the centre of the country out to the territorial waters, from the earth below our feet to the heavens above. Any landowner, no matter how small or large, has a right of exclusive possession of land 'a caelo usque ad centrum' (from the sky to the centre of the earth). But this possession is not absolute, it is conditional. Under feudalism the rights enjoyed by an owner are determined by the nature of his or her title which in turn is derived from his or her 'superior'. Ultimately all the land of Scotland is held by God, the divine authority invoked by the Crown (the Paramount Superior) in Scotland to claim the territory of Scotland. Most land in Scotland is held under feudal tenure and therefore under the Crown as Paramount Superior. Exceptions include land in Orkney and Shetland together with other land such as church glebes which are held as alloidal land (or udal land in the Northern Isles). Here the Crown has no direct feudal interest (although the land, in common with the rest of the country, comes under the sovereign authority of the Scottish Crown) and land is held outright by the owner.

Under feudal tenure, landowners who hold their land directly from the Crown are known as vassals. Such vassals may themselves become feudal superiors by retaining certain rights and imposing certain obligations on those to whom they sell, or feu, land. Such people, in turn may become superiors through further retention and imposition of rights on other new owners who become their vassals. There is no limit to the number of times this process, known as feuing or subinfeudation may occur and it adds a further dimension of ownership to that associated with the actual occupation of land.

Land which is sold need not of course be feud and can be sold outright. Whilst the process of subinfeudation creates a new feudal estate and a new superior-vassal relationship with the former vassal now becoming a superior whilst still being a vassal of his or her superior, outright sale of land to another owner merely substitutes the interests of one vassal for another (or one superior for another).

The system is archaic, complex and open to abuse and for over 30 years there have been enquiries and reports designed finally to lead to abolition. Some modest legislation flowed from these enquiries but it is only now that abolition is, finally, beginning to be translated into legislative action.[5]

Feuing, which became widespread in the 16th century, was a hugely beneficial process for superiors who enjoyed a substantial initial cash payment together with an ongoing annual fixed payment. In a relationship which was really in practice a tenancy, the superior could resume the feu at the end of the term and had the power to approve or otherwise who should inherit the feu. This was the basic relationship which survived until 1747 and which enabled the great landed families of Scotland to 'have their cake and eat it'.

In addition, as feudalism developed, the remaining lands of the Crown and the Church, which had substantially disappeared by the end of the 16th century, were absorbed by the landed aristocracy. Not content with such riches, they then embarked on a programme of law reform (of course, they made the law), which consolidated and strengthened their power and rights. In the 17th century, for example, the bulk of the legislation in the Scots Parliament was concerned with the ownership and use of land. The Register of Sasines, which gave greater security to land titles, was established in 1617 and the law of entail, introduced in 1685, prevented land from being lost when a landowner went bankrupt.

Having secured the vast bulk of the former lands of the Crown and the Church by the end of the 16th century, landowners turned their attention to the third great land grab – the commonties. These were originally areas of genuine common land, amounting to millions of acres, which survived the first five centuries of feudalism. In a series of Acts of the Scots Parliament they were redefined as a form of private property, the rights to which were held to be shared by all neighbouring landowners. In 1695 an Act was passed allowing for their division and appropriation into the hands of Scotland's landed elites. Even that land which was controlled by local burghs was systematically pillaged. As historian and politician Tom Johnston so eloquently put it:

'Until the Burgh Reform Act of 1833 the landowners and the commercial bourgeois class controlled all burghal administration of the common lands, and controlled it in such a way that vast areas of common lands were quietly appropriated, trust funds wholly disappeared, and to such a length did the plunder and the corruption develop, that some ancient burghs with valuable patrimonies went bankrupt, some disappeared altogether from the map of Scotland, some had their charters confiscated, and those which survived to the middle of the 19th century were left mere miserable starved caricatures of their former greatness, their Common Good funds gone, their lands fenced in private ownership, and their treasurers faced often with crushing debts.'[8]

'As late as 1800 there were great common properties extant; many burghs, towns and villages owned lands and mosses; Forres engaged in municipal timber-growing; Fortrose owned claypits; Glasgow owned quarries and coalfields; Hamilton owned a coal pit; Irvine had mills, farms and a loom shop... '[9]

The 1695 act allowing for the division of commonties was part of a wider body of 17th-century legislation aimed at rationalising and clarifying the hold of landowners on their land. The momentum for this was reflected in the re-concentration in the pattern of landownership that started during that century. By the end of the 17th century there were around 9,500 landowners in Scotland, only around half of whom had the right to inherit or sell the land they held.[10] By the mid 1800s there were around 8,500 and, by the end of the 19th century, around 8,000. During that period Scotland's population had grown from 1 to 1.5 million and the percentage of them owning land had therefore fallen from 1 per cent to 0.5 per cent.

The 1830s and 1840s were a watershed in the social geography of Scotland as the overall population balance tipped to being urban rather than rural. In a countryside populated overwhelmingly by a tenantry with no security, landowners' power remained unchallenged. As the century wore on, their prosperity increased, fuelled by rents from land and minerals and from the lucrative feus of land for urban and industrial development. But the high point of Victorian landed prosperity was about to be challenged: in the late 1800s there was an upsurge of unrest and agitation from an increasingly oppressed and poverty-stricken peasantry.

LAND TENURE IN THE HIGHLANDS & ISLANDS

Considerable confusion surrounds the introduction of feudalism into the Highlands and Islands of Scotland. It is often popularly claimed that feudalism was introduced following the Jacobite defeat at Culloden and replaced older forms of communal and kinship tenure. This is wrong. Feudalism, whilst slower to penetrate this region, was nevertheless present from an early stage. The difference lay in the limited significance which was generally attached to feudal authority by clan chiefs who generally respected older Celtic traditions and relationships based on kinship relations. Crown authority was quite simply less well developed in parts of the Highlands than it was in the Lowlands. As the feudal system of political authority spread throughout Scotland in the 12th century, clan chiefs in the Highlands and Islands were noticeably slower to submit to the authority of the Scottish Crown than their Lowland Scotland counterparts. Whilst Lowland Scotland was under the full control of the Crown by the end of the 13th century, it took until the end of the 15th century for most Highland chiefs to obtain Crown charters to their lands.

But by the end of the 16th century following a 1598 Act requiring all owners in the Highlands to produce their title deeds, few landowners could ignore the political wisdom of obtaining a feudal charter. In a region of contested loyalties and often violent territorial conflict a Crown charter could provide a useful safeguard against the unwelcome claims of neighbours. Contrary to some popular views, therefore, clan chiefs were by this time legally just as much feudal landowners as their contemporaries in Lowland Scotland although with Crown authority weak, landownership in the region was left as something of a hybrid institution between two very different sets of assumptions.

All this was to change in the social, economic and political upheavals of the 17th and 18th centuries. Highland society's faith in the endurance of older understandings of land tenure was shattered as clan chiefs exercised their feudal authority and sold land to people with very different ideas about community relations, some of whom subsequently authorised the clearances which to this day endure as a manifestation of the despotism of much Highland landlordism at this time.

Revolution

Before exploring some of what happened in that period it is worth pausing to reflect on how and why Scotland remained in the grip of feudal power at a time when all over Europe it was being swept away with revolutionary alacrity.[11]

The political revolutions in Europe were concerned with the dismantling of feudal regimes in which the ownership of land and the exercise of political power were still both in the hands of absolute monarchs. Frustration and anger at the iniquity and injustice of serfdom led to political uprisings, the consequences of which were both the reform of political power structures and the reform of landownership. Out of this process emerged the peasant proprietor and, from the dismantling of Crown and Church estates, the extensive communally owned lands of western Europe.

Scotland missed out on all of this – why? A key factor was the 1688 Glorious Revolution in England and the 1689 Claim of Right in Scotland. These effectively wrested political power from the Crown. Following the Union of 1707, the Scottish nobility in partnership with the English possessed the political power, the landed power, and the military power. It was a force against which a peasant uprising was never going to succeed, as a number of failed attempts in the 18th and 19th centuries were to prove.

The political power of European peasants in the 19th century was never to be enjoyed by those who lived on the land in Scotland. They suffered the consequences in the Clearances and gravitated towards the slums of industrial Scotland, whilst their counterparts in Scandinavia and western Europe, though poor, at least had land. The heirs to that land today are the prosperous small proprietors scattered throughout the Norwegian, French, German and Dutch countryside.

The disempowered peasantry of Scotland was provided
with a path other than political agitation – serfdom in
the coal mines and factories of industrial Scotland and
living in the slums associated with them. In the country,
a waged labouring class found employment on farms
and estates. Periodically, they were drawn or dragooned
into serving the British Empire overseas and required to
be prepared to lay their lives on the line for a
Government which turned a blind eye on evictions and
the clearance of the family's holding back home.

The British Empire also provided the wealth with which
a new strata of landowners emerged from the lesser
nobility and bourgeoisie. The 19th century was the high
point of landed power when, despite the weakening of
the links between land and political power heralded by
the extension of the franchise through the Reform Acts,
landowners remained free to exploit their land as they
saw fit and to evict and variously manipulate the
population at will.

The economic depression of the 1870s and 1880s
brought rural discontent to a head. A number of
political organisations were formed to campaign for
land reform, among them the Highland Land League,
the Scottish Land Restoration League and the Scottish
Land Reform Alliance. Much has been written about
the Highland Land League and crofter agitation in the
north and west Highlands but demands for reform came
from all over Scotland, notably the North-East.

The Scottish Land Reform Alliance was the main
organisation in Scotland pushing for land reform.
It demanded abolition of hypothec, entails and
primogeniture, the reform of game laws, tenants' rights
of compensation, and the granting of secure and
heritable agricultural tenancies. Inspired by the earlier
efforts of the Chartist Land Plan and the National Land
Company, movements such as the Commercial Land

Company emerged, aimed at organising the break-up of large landholdings and the creation of peasant holdings.[12] But the collapse of Gladstone's government in 1894, and the convolutions of Irish Home Rule, contributed to the lack of success of these movements and of the agitators and campaigners of the wider land reform movement such as the Crofters Party.

The 20th Century

By the beginning of the 20th century political attention was increasingly focused on the land question, but reforms such as the 1886 Crofters' Holdings Act, although posing a serious challenge to landowners, were confined to the Highlands. In the Lowlands, landed power avoided becoming a focus for popular resistance in the 19th century due to the ready availability of jobs in the growing industrial centres where radical politics was channelled into the developing labour movement.

The Highlands was in the vanguard of land reform during this time. This was as much to do with the weaker political power of landowners in the region, as with the strength of the Highland peasants' case for some redress. Incidentally, Aberdeenshire was left out of the Crofting Act of 1886, despite meeting all the criteria for inclusion, for no better a reason than that the Napier Commission had not visited it![13]

Continued unrest and demands for more land by Highland crofters in particular led to legislation in 1911 (The Small Landholders Act), which extended crofting tenure to the rest of Scotland. It was too little too late for the Lowland peasantry but it did, in contrast to the Crofters Act, stimulate landed interests to get better organised politically.

Until the beginning of the 20th century, landowners were in little need of any structured organisation to represent their interests. Their status as part of the ruling elite negated the need for more formalised arrangements. But as land reform initiated at the end of the 19th century gained momentum, landowners began to feel the need to organise themselves. In November 1906, on the back of a furious outcry by landowners over the Small Landholders Bill, the Scottish Land & Property Federation was formed to protect landowners' interests. The proposals, which eventually became law in 1911, were defeated by the House of Lords twice and were only passed after the Lords veto had been abolished in May 1911. This abolition, it is worth noting, was in response to the rejection by the Lords of Lloyd George's budget of 1909 which proposed the introduction of land taxes.

These events, culminating in the Land Settlement (Scotland) Act of 1919, marked the the last attempt at serious land reform in Scotland, although the Agricultural Holdings Act 1949 which gave tenant farmers security of tenure was significant.

The remainder of the 20th century has witnessed an expansion of owner-occupied farming in the 1920s and 1930s, the development of the social or not-for-profit landownership sector from the 1930s with the purchase by the National Trust for Scotland of Glencoe and Dalness,[14] and a phase of rapid expansion of state-owned land in the 1950s and 1960s. It has also seen the slow but steady break up of the large estates of the landed aristocracy. In the period between 1912 and 1920, land agents Knight Frank and Rutley alone had sold 1.6 million acres of Scotland.[15]

During the 20th century major incursions of statutory law have been made into the private affairs of landowners, most notably in the fields of planning and the environment. But the institution of landed power remains for all that formidable and effective. A body of property law built up over the centuries remains in place as a bulwark against any radical change in the pattern of landownership. Even feudal reform, heavily promoted by reforming politicians will do nothing to alter the basic division of land in the Scottish countryside.

For all but 17 of the 55 post-war years the UK has been governed by the traditional party of the landed gentry, the Tories. Pressure for change has been present but has been marginalised and suppressed by institutional inertia, opposition from Government and hostility from landed interests.

Land is power, and the current system of land tenure and division of land is a direct consequence of how that power has been defined and distributed in past centuries.

A democratic mandate has never been sought for the way in which Scotland's land is owned. By the time universal suffrage was introduced in 1928 the basic land laws and the division of land had all been established. Land is power, and the current system of land tenure and division of land is a direct consequence of how that power has been defined and distributed in past centuries.

The history of landed power in Scotland is a history of a class whose authority and hegemony have never been challenged effectively, whose possession of disproportionate property holdings has never been broken, and whose influence on debates on landownership and use has been conspicuous by its formidable extent and discrete application.

Thankfully that *may* all be about to change.

REFERENCES

Note: Full references are given in 'Further Reading' at the end of the book.

1. Marx. *The Eighteenth Brumaire of Louis Bonaparte.*
2. Johnston. *Our Scots Noble Families.*
3. Lord Sewel, Foreword to Scottish Office, 1999.
4. Sir John Sinclair, 1814.
5. Scottish Law Commission, 1999

6. For a thorough and authoritative history of how the pattern of landownership in Scotland evolved, see Callander, 1987. Much of the factual material in this chapter is derived from this book.

7. Massey & Alejandrina, 1978, p. 186.
8. Johnston, *Working Classes,* p. 163.
9. Johnston, *Working Classes,* p. 389.
10. Callander, *Pattern of Landownership,* p. 44.
11. Hobsbawm, *Age of Revolution.* Chapter 8, Land.
12. See Boyd (1998) for a history of these social movements and Wightman (1996a) and Boyd & Reid (1999) for an up-to-date assessment of the not-for-profit sector in the late 20th century.
13. Carter, *Farm Life,* p. 171
14. Boyd, 1998.
15. Cannadine, 1990, p. 109

Chapter 2
Scotland – A Feudal Land at the Onset of a New Millennium

If Scotland is to enjoy a programme of land reform which emancipates its citizens, the underlying features of the current division of land and system of land tenure will need to be analysed, understood and reformed. What characterises Scottish landownership at the end of the 20th century is a system of land law and distribution of land which has been consigned to the museums of rural life in the rest of western Europe. It is further characterised by a fiscal regime and land market which is liberal in the extreme and which has conferred vast power over huge swathes of countryside on a tiny number of people.

The Pattern of Landownership in Scotland

Derived from Wightman (1996b), Wightman (1998) and other unpublished data.

Scotland	19,068,631 acres	100%
Urban	585,627 acres	3%
Rural	18,483,004 acres	97%

Of the rural land, 2,275,768 acres are in the ownership of public bodies

and 16,207,236 are in the ownership of private bodies.

Of this privately-owned rural land:

One quarter is owned by 66 landowners in estates of 30,700 acres and larger

One third is owned by 120 landowners in estates of 21,000 acres and larger

One half is owned by 343 landowners in estates of 7,500 acres and larger

Two thirds is owned by 1,252 landowners in estates of 1,200 acres and larger

---

Table 1

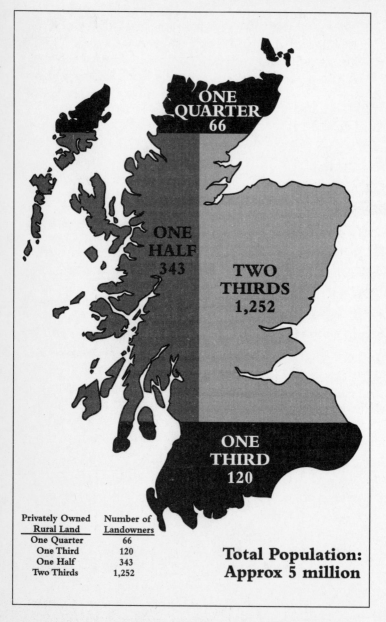

Privately Owned Rural Land	Number of Landowners
One Quarter	66
One Third	120
One Half	343
Two Thirds	1,252

Total Population: Approx 5 million

Research has yet to reveal a country anywhere in the world with such a concentrated pattern of private landownership.

The statistics speak for themselves. In a country of 19 million acres and 5 million people, a mere 1,252 landowners (0.025 per cent of the population) own two-thirds of the privately-owned rural land (Table 1). This manifest inequity in how land has been divided – its value pocketed, its use ill-judged, its ownership carefully protected and defended, and its inhabitants harshly treated over the centuries – lies at the heart of the land question and its potency as a political issue.

And it is this manifest discrepancy in how land has been divided, how its value pocketed, its use so ill-judged, its ownership so carefully protected and defended, and its inhabitants so harshly treated over the centuries that lies at the heart of the land and its potency as a political issue.

Scotland's present landowners may not be directly responsible for bringing about the iniquitous state of affairs which constitutes landownership in Scotland today. But they are responsible for the continued defence of the system, for their denial that it is indeed iniquitous, for their exploitation of every available means to avoid paying tax, for their manipulation of the subsidy system, for the distortion of the land market, and for the continued promotion of their own vested interests in important matters of public interest.

So how does the land lie today? Well, as the Scottish Parliament prepares to abolish Scotland's antiquated system of land tenure, perhaps it is best to start with feudalism itself.

The End of Feudalism

Feudalism is the basic framework which, over time, has been adapted by the more powerful landowners at any point in history so as to sustain their own vested interests. Consideration of current proposals to abolish feudal tenure will be given later, but here it is worth noting that as feudal influence has weakened over the centuries, other aspects of Scotland's property laws (such as the laws of entail, of trust, of succession, and of game rights) have been consolidated and strengthened. So much so, that the final abolition of feudalism after almost 900 years will actually have negligible impact either on landowners, or on the pattern of landownership in Scotland.

What is left of the feudal system is a skeletal framework. Real power in property lies in other aspects of Scots property law. Feudalism is a quaint anachronism which, given the potency of the terms superior and vassal, landed interests are actually amongst the keenest to see swept away.

The Pattern of Landownership

Scotland may not be characterised by feudal tenure for much longer but its abolition poses no real threat to the current division of land. And it is this division of land, the most concentrated pattern of private land ownership in Europe (more concentrated even than in countries such as Brazil) which is at the root of most of the problems which land reform seeks to address. Success in doing so will depend on the extent to which it challenges and changes this division of land rather than merely solving some of the more obvious symptoms which such a pattern gives rise to. Table 1 illustrates the severity of the problem. In parts of the country the pattern is even more concentrated. In the Highlands and Islands fully half of the private land – over 3.6 million acres – is owned by fewer than 100 landowners and three-quarters of it is owned by around 300.

This pattern of ownership stands in stark contrast to other west European countries where typically, the pattern is around 1,000 times less concentrated and where communal forms of ownership are commonplace.

Landed Hegemony

Such a pattern is remarkable in itself, but what is even more astonishing is the way in which the landowning establishment itself is not merely a collection of random individuals but a tightly-knit network of power and influence extending into the fields of politics and finance. The small numbers involved facilitate the operation of this network and its effectiveness which extend to the highest levels of British society.

The preponderance of double-barrelled names in the aristocracy (Dingwall-Fordyce, Strang-Steel, Gordon-Duff-Pennington, Ogilvie-Grant-Nicholson, Buchanan-Jardine, Douglas-Home, Heriot-Maitland, Forbes-Leith, Macpherson-Grant, Campbell-Preston) is testimony to the practice of inter-marriage among the landed classes. Almost all of the traditional landed families of Scotland are related to each other, linked together in a web of kinship that has built up over centuries. Strategic marriages consolidated different holdings within the same wider family grouping and strengthened the grip of the landed classes on the institution of landownership. The result is the following tangled web of power and influence, starting with the Queen Mother herself. (All those named own land in Scotland.)

The Queen Mother is the daughter of the 14th Earl of Strathmore. Her sister was married to the 4th Earl of Granville, whose granddaughter, Lady Marcia is married to Jonathan Bulmer. The 2nd Earl of Granville's daughter was the grandmother of James Morrison, Lord Margadale. Princess Antonia von Preusen, another relative of the Queen, is married to the Marquess of Duoro whose father is the 8th Duke of Wellington. The Queen's former private secretary is Lord Charteris of Amisfield, whose daughter is married to Lord Pearson of Rannoch. Lord Charteris's brother is the 12th Earl of Wemyss and March, whose daughter, Lady Elizabeth

Charteris is married to David Holford Benson,
Chairman of Kleinwort Charter Investment Trust. A
former Chairman of Kleinwort Benson Group
(1993–96) itself is Baron Rockley who is married to the
elder daughter of 7th Earl of Cadogan. The Queen is
also related to the Earl of Airlie through his brother, Sir
Angus Ogilvy who is married to Princess Alexandra of
Kent. The Countess of Airlie is also a Lady to the
Bedchamber of the Queen. The Earl of Airlie was
Chairman of Schroders merchant bank from 1977 to
1984, whilst Bruno Schroder himself owns Dunlossit
Estate on Islay next door to Lord Margadale! Another
relative of the Queen, James Hamilton, the 5th Duke of
Abercorn is married to Alexandra Anastasia, whose
niece is married to the Duke of Westminster. The Duke's
sister, Lady Jane Grosvenor, was the first wife of the
Duke of Roxburghe (Her marriage to Roxburghe made
her the daughter of a Duke, the sister of a Duke, the
wife of a Duke and finally the mother of a future
Duke!). Meanwhile the Queen's aunt, the Duchess of
Gloucester, is the 3rd daughter of the 7th Duke of
Buccleuch whose widow is the daughter of the 13th Earl
of Home. The current Duke of Buccleuch's sister is the
Duchess of Northumberland whose daughter was the
first wife of the Duke of Sutherland. The Duke of
Buccleuch's son and heir is Richard Walter John
Montague Douglas Scott, the Earl of Dalkeith. Richard
is married to Lady Elizabeth Kerr, the youngest
daughter of the 12th Marquess of Lothian. Lady
Elizabeth's sister, Lady Cecil Kerr, is married to Donald
Cameron of Locheil (younger). The hereditary master of
the Queen's household in Scotland is Ian Campbell, the
12th Duke of Argyll who is married to the daughter of
Sir Ivar Colquhoun of Luss whose nephew is Sir
Michael Wigan. Sir Ivar's sister is the widow of the 8th
Earl of Arran. The great-grandson of the 4th Earl of
Arran's brother married the daughter of the 4th Earl of

Cawdor. Going back to Donald Cameron for a minute –
his grandmother was the daughter of the 5th Duke of
Montrose whose son, the 6th Duke, was the father of
Lady Jean Fforde, the mother of Charles Fforde from
Arran. The 6th Duke's niece married the late Thomas
Campbell-Preston whose half-sister is Sarah Troughton.
Thomas's father, Robert Campbell-Preston was married
to Angela Pearson, the 3rd daughter of 2nd Viscount
Cowdray and the mother (by her first marriage) of the
late Duke of Atholl. A scion of the Atholl Murrays is
the Earl of Mansfield whose sister is married to the 20th
Earl of Moray. Meanwhile the Atholl Estates factor,
Andrew Gordon, is also the factor for Robin Fleming,
whose cousin, Dorothy Fleming (who married his
brother, Major Richard Fleming), together with her
sister Mrs Schuster (and husband Richard Schuster), are
also Argyllshire landowners. Robert was chairman of
Robert Fleming Holdings from 1990 to 1997 of which
Henry Keswick is also a Director. Henry and his
youngest brother Simon are Chairman and Director of
Jardine Matheson Holdings Ltd. (whose founder, James
Matheson, at one time owned the Island of Lewis). At
least six other Dumfriesshire landowners have close
connections with Jardine Matheson. Henry is married to
Tessa, Lady Reay, younger daughter of the late Lord
Lovat whilst Henry's other brother, Sir John 'Chips'
Keswick, Chairman of Hambro's Bank, is married to
Lady Sarah Ramsay, daughter of the 16th Earl of
Dalhousie who himself was related to the Lovats
through his wife whose mother was the daughter of the
13th Lord Lovat. The late 16th Earl of Dalhousie's
cousin is Captain Ramsay of Mar and his late mother
was Lady Mary Heathcote-Drummond-Willoughby,
daughter of the 1st Earl of Ancaster. Her great niece is
Baroness Jane Heathcote-Drummond-Willoughby de
Eresby whose grandfather on her mother's side was the
2nd Viscount Astor. The second son of the 1st Viscount

Ah Charles – I hear your daughter's marrying old
Sir Godfrey's son. Nice to know the rest of the county is going to
be in such safe hands and I guess we can count on you to help
fight these ridiculous land reform plans!

Astor was the 1st Baron Astor of Hever whose grandson is Philip Astor. Philip's sister, the Honourable Sarah Violet Astor is married to George Lopes. The first Baron Astor's wife was the mother of the Marquess of Landsdowne and the daughter of the 4th Earl of Minto. The son and heir of the Marquess is the Earl of Shelbourne whose brother is Lord Robert Mercer-Nairne, someone who, as we will see, has some interesting views on tenant farming.

That lot own over 12 per cent of the private land in Scotland! This pattern of influence and landed power has lasted right up until the very end of the 20th century, bolstered by wider networks within politics, finance and the law. Such intimate relationships promote social cohesion among landowners, which makes them readily distinguishable today as a discrete class with its own values, internal networks, and related social institutions.

How has such a situation arisen? A number of legal, fiscal and social devices have been deployed. Understanding these is critical to developing a programme of land reform, as it is only by changing these factors, where possible, that the current system can begin to be dismantled.

Property Law
Scotland's property laws have been devised and manipulated to cement and sustain landowning power. Given that title to so much land was originally obtained by corruption and theft, such legitimacy was desperately needed. Property laws have historically been constructed to legitimise the exercise of naked aggression, larceny and corruption.[1]

Nowhere is this more evident that the law of prescription whereby land held without challenge becomes owned by whoever is first to stake a recognised legal claim. Not only is this a handy device for wealthy landowners who can afford good legal advice, but the persistent concentrated pattern of private ownership of the last 900 years of feudalism would not have been possible without it. It has also been highly successful in effecting the transformation of common property into private property.

Other tools of the land tenure system are the powers of pre-emption and redemption. These enable landowners to have their cake and eat it by feuing land and being able to reacquire it either at their own discretion or at the occurrence of a specific event (in the case of redemption), or having a power of first refusal if and when the vassal wishes to sell (pre-emption). These powers still exist, although reduced in effectiveness.

Other property laws covering, for example, game rights and access, have also been instrumental in creating the institution of private landownership which exists in Scotland today. Such laws were, of course, made by landowners.

Politics

Througout the 18th and 19th centuries the House of Lords and the House of Commons were dominated by landed interests. Parliament has its formal opening in November because historically the Monarch, peers and ministers were too busy shooting things in the Scottish Highlands during August, September and October. Members of the House of Lords and Commons have made the laws (and not made others) which underpin the current system and pattern of landownership in Scotland.

It is this institution which created the political and economic climate for the British Empire and for the invasion of so many overseas countries. It was this institution which made sure that the political emancipation which heralded the end of feudalism in much of western Europe never took hold in Britain until well into the 20th century. Above all, it has been this institution which has maintained a stranglehold on the ownership of land in Scotland and ensured that the legal framework surrounding landed property continues to reflect the vested interests of its members.

Wealth

In the 17th century land became as much a commercial and financial asset as a political one hence the extent of legislation designed to consolidate and protect its ownership. At this time, for example, debts on property could be bought from creditors by another landowner who was then entitled to claim the property – a process known as apprisal. This process was resented by the landowning classes and a series of Acts were passed limiting its use.

This led to the 1685 Law of Entail whereby an estate could be 'entailed' and thus protected against forced sale by creditors. Entailment became more widespread as a means of securing the line of succession and preventing the break up of estates in the event of bankruptcy or similar misfortune. It eventually became more trouble than it was worth, however, since it reduced the flexibility available to heirs although new entails could be created until 1914 and some estates remain entailed today. Over the period, however, other more appropriate devices have been introduced which achieve many of the same objects but with greater flexibility.

Private trusts are one such device for protecting estates against unforeseen taxation and of securing the line of succession to land. At least one fifth of all private land in Scotland is now held in private trusts. These protect land from, among other things, inheritance tax and they can determine future succession to the estate. It is a device which also distorts the land market through the withholding of land from normal exposure over several generations.

Landowning power has also sustained itself throughout economically difficult times by exploiting the rising land values throughout the 18th, 19th and 20th centuries as urban Scotland expanded. The wealth accumulated by the handful of families who owned the land on which Edinburgh, Glasgow, Dundee, Aberdeen and Scotland's new towns now stand has kept them in a style to which no one else is or has been accustomed.

The legacy of the 18th and 19th century bonanza in development can be seen in city street names that commemorate the original landowners, many of whom still possess substantial feudal estates in urban Scotland. The country houses of the Lowlands were not financed simply from rents drawn from agriculture and minerals (though that was important), but on the continuous stream of capital receipts gained from selling land for development.

The introduction of the Town and Country Planning Act in 1947 seriously threatened this milch cow. Landowners demanded compensation for the loss of development rights (and got it) but any disadvantage suffered was soon more than recompensed by the increased scarcity value which land (by now requiring planning consent) enjoyed. The purchase and sale of land for speculative development purposes increased, with specialised development companies often taking the place of traditional landowners in the development of the urban fringe.

Inheritance

Throughout most of Europe the laws governing how land is inherited were reformed in the 18th and 19th centuries as part of the abolition of feudalism and the removal of the principle of primogeniture whereby land is inherited by the first born male to the exclusion of all others. The reforms were made to allow more than just the eldest son to inherit property and were almost exclusively responsible for the pattern of small-scale owner-occupation now prevalent across western Europe.

Of course, such a policy has also been responsible for the fragmentation of holdings, to the extent that they become both unviable and administratively cumbersome. To overcome this, however, sophisticated programmes of land consolidation have been developed to restructure holdings.

succession law has been probably the most important non-feudal element of property law which has perpetuated the concentrated pattern of private landownership in Scotland.

In Scotland the only reform in the law of succession to land in recent years was in 1964, when primogeniture was finally abolished and when spouses and children obtained legal rights to inherit the family home (but not any land). Otherwise nothing has changed and landowners have consistently resisted any reform in the law to widen the legal rights to inherit land as this would not only begin the process of breaking up large landholdings but would seriously dilute the social structure whereby eldest sons still tend to inherit land at the expense of women in general and other children in particular.

Thus, succession law has been probably the most important non-feudal element of property law which has perpetuated the concentrated pattern of private landownership in Scotland.

Tax
Not content with drawing rent and capital receipts, shielding them from creditors and securing their inheritance, landed interests throughout Britain have consistently exploited and promoted measures designed

to limit the exposure of their wealth to taxation.
Moreover, with the abolition of sporting rates in 1995,
land in Scotland now attracts no annual tax burden for
the first time in nearly a millennium.

Surreptitiously the overall tax burden has shifted from
landowners to waged labour, investments and savings.
This, as many economists point out, is the root cause of
much economic misery as rising public expenditure
demands an increased slice of the earned wealth in the
economy as opposed to the unearned wealth (of which
land values are a substantial component).

The dukes, earls and marquesses bemoan the effects of
inheritance tax and death duties on large estates even
although such taxes can be avoided easily and thus are
largely regarded as voluntary taxes. Never mind too that
there has been an overwhelming shift in the burden of
taxation away from landowners to working people. Even
where tax still bites, many of Scotland's leading families
have hidden the beneficial ownership of the land behind
nominee companies and offshore trusts so as to avoid the
penetration of the Inland Revenue. The truth is that, as in
the past, the accumulation of wealth through landed
estates still defies the efforts of government to promote
greater equity and fairness in the distribution of what is,
after all, often unearned wealth.

The Unregulated Market

A feature of the land market in Britain as a whole is its
remarkably unregulated nature. In other countries in
Europe regulation in one form or another exists in order
to promote certain social policies (e.g. the retention of
the family farm). By contrast, anyone from anywhere
can buy as much land as they like in Scotland. A legacy
of Britain's imperial past (in order to expand abroad, it
had to concede rights to foreigners to buy land here), its
wider impact has been to prevent any regulation to
control the domestic land market.

Landed interests in Scotland oppose vehemently any regulation which restricts their freedom to buy and sell land. Such a lack of regulation means that, for example, offshore trusts abound, absentee landownership is permissible and sales can take place in private and free of any public scrutiny. Such a lack of regulation is often referred to as a free market in land. By definition there is no free market in land. It is fixed in supply and therefore is incapable of responding to demand. This means that a form of monopoly ownership exists whereby current owners control when and how much land comes on the market.

Conclusions

The situation today in Scotland is one where the land is held in the stranglehold of a tiny minority whose hold over it has been afforded by the various legal and fiscal protections historically available to them. Elsewhere their role has been taken over by a various assorted rabble of the nouveau riche, speculators, offshore companies, and other institutions who have taken possession by means of a market in land which allows anyone from anywhere to buy as much land as they like, no questions asked.

In the absence of any meaningful reform of this situation, landowning hegemony has persisted in much of Scotland whilst a destructive, disempowering and corrupt regime of neo-feudalism has emerged under the modern potentates who exercise power over great swathes of the Scottish countryside (in the Highlands in particular).

In rural Scotland, two-thirds of households have incomes below the Low Pay Unit Poverty Threshold. Rural Scotland has the most concentrated, inequitable pattern of private landed property anywhere in Europe. Scotland too is the last country in the modern world still to have feudal tenure. And this is no coincidence. In

rural Scotland there persists a pattern of poverty and
homelessness which is every bit as offensive as that
which exists in urban Scotland.[2] Both have their roots
in a system of land tenure, a division of land, and a
fiscal system which benefit a fortunate few at the
expense of the many.

But perhaps this is not a problem or, if it is, perhaps it is
readily resolved. Here the debate can become confusing
since there are contested interpretations and definitions
of what land reform means. So, before developing a
meaningful programme of land reform, it is worth
exploring in some detail what is meant by the term.

REFERENCES

1. See Johnston, 1909 for more in this vein!

2. Corbett & Logie, 1997 and Corbett & Wightman, 1998.

Chapter 3
So What is Land Reform?

The first man who enclosed a piece of ground and found people simple enough to believe him was the real founder of civil society.

JEAN-JACQUES ROUSSEAU[1]

The impact of the land tenure system goes far beyond land use. It influences the size and distribution of an area's population; the labour skills and the entrepreneurial experiences of the population; access to employment and thus migration; access to housing; access to land to build new houses; the social structure; and the distribution of power and influence. In many areas of rural Scotland, large landowners play a crucial role in local development: they are the rural planners.

BRYAN MCGREGOR,
Professor of Land Economy at Aberdeen University[2]

Classical land reform, namely the redistribution of larger agricultural holdings among the landless population, has taken place in many parts of the world, inspired by liberation and revolutionary movements, particularly in socialist countries in the developing world such as Mexico in 1920, China in 1949, Cuba in 1962, Peru 1968–75, Nicaragua in 1981, and currently in South Africa.[3] Major global institutions such as the UN and World Bank have also supported and promoted land reform in various countries and regions.

Land reform in a post-industrial country like Scotland poses unique questions in an age where agriculture is in decline but where, as James Hunter, the Highland historian, pointed out recently,[4] the rural population, rather than declining as was the case 150 years ago, is now growing. Scotland is in a phase of development where technological advances and the growth of the service sector might be regarded as negating any need for reform of that primary resource, land.

But land, though it may not be of such great importance agriculturally, is still the basic resource upon which settlement, infrastructure and development of all kinds depend. In Scotland, access to that resource remains in too many places limited through the wilful obstinance, greed or simple neglect of landowners whose power to determine who, where, how and when land use change will take place remains formidable by virtue of feudal and non-feudal land laws and because of the vast extent over which such power prevails and is exercised.

The problem is most acute in those areas away from the urban centres where land markets are least well developed, where large landholdings predominate and where (a certain paternalism notwithstanding) too many landowners are disinterested in the social and economic aspirations of other people in the community.

But to focus exclusively on rural land would be misguided. That would ignore the immense rental and capital values tied up in urban land which pose specifically urban problems in terms of access to land. Problems of affordable housing, public amenity, congestion and poverty are associated with how land is owned and used in urban areas just as much as in rural areas.

What is Land?

Land is a physical resource. It is the territory we occupy, including the ground beneath our feet, the skies above our heads, the inland water, and territorial seas. It is defined legally as the territory over which Scots law has jurisdiction.

In its broadest sense land reform is concerned with changing the way in which society relates to the ownership and to the use of land. This can be broken down into four simple components:

> how the land is owned (the system of land tenure)
>
> the pattern of ownership

who owns the land

how the land is used.

Conceptually these relationships can be thought of as different aspects of power relationships within society.

how land is owned	=	derivation of power
pattern of ownership	=	distribution of power
who owns land	=	holders of power
how land is used	=	exercise of power

But before we get into this in more detail, let's look at the main inspirations and motivations for land reform. A range of philosophical approaches to land has developed over the years. Land has been a core element in economic, political, environmental and spiritual thinking.

The Economic Discourse

Land has historically been regarded as a distinctive part of the economy. The classical economists such as Adam Smith and John Stuart Mill argued that economic growth arising from the deployment of land, labour and capital was to be encouraged but that land, unlike labour and capital, was fixed in supply and therefore subject to monopoly control by landowners.

Most economists have, to a greater or lesser degree, recognised the special and unique features of land in the economy. The Physiocrats certainly did, likewise social reformers Henry George, William Ogilvie and Patrick Dove, and even modern economists such as Friedrich von Hayek and Milton Friedman have acknowledged the fact, albeit fleetingly.

Monopoly control of land can be regarded as a failure of capitalism to respond to emerging demands placed on land – what Marx referred to as primitive accumulation.

'So-called primitive accumulation', he argued, '... is nothing else than the historical process of divorcing the producer from the means of production. It appears "primitive" because it forms the pre-history of capital, and of the mode of production corresponding to capital.'

'In the history of primitive accumulation, all revolutions are epoch-making that act as levers for the capitalist class in its formation; but this is true above all for those moments when great masses of men are suddenly and forcibly torn from their means of subsistence, and hurled onto the labour market as free, unprotected and rightless proletarians. The expropriation of the agricultural producer, of the peasant, from the soil is the basis of the whole process. The history of this expropriation assumes different aspects in different countries, and runs through its different phases in different orders of succession, and at different historical epochs.'[5]

This process, as Marx himself understood, was not intrinsic to the logic of that mode of value-creation called capitalism. Paying money to buy land from owners out of capital was a systematic contradiction to capitalism. Even the most laissez-faire of economists, Friedrich von Hayek, Milton Friedman and Martin Feldstein do not seriously dispute this.[6]

And such a perspective has a bearing on land reform today. To obtain a house plot in rural Scotland can cost £20,000 just for a quarter acre that has lain there for thousands of years undeveloped and unused save for a few sheep. There is no shortage of land. Arguably there should be no market for quarter-acre building plots – one should be able to pick them up almost as freely as the seaweed. Restricting the supply of land through monopoly landownership and through planning restrictions forces up land prices artificially, limiting the

To obtain a house plot in rural Scotland can cost £20,000 just for a quarter acre that has lain there for thousands of years undeveloped and unused save for a few sheep.

scope for economic growth and disproportionately advantaging landowners and speculators at the expense of the rest of society.

The Political Discourse

The ownership of land, as well as conferring economic power, confers political power – the privilege of being able to decide how land is to be used and thus whether and when the wider community's aspirations can be met. The historical development of how political power has been held and exercised is intimately tied up with the way in which land has been owned and distributed. As historian Loretta Timperley observed, 'Power and landownership have been synonymous in Scotland from time immemorial'.[7]

Access to land, control of land, ownership of land have all been central issues of political revolutions, autonomy movements and political high drama the world over. This is not surprising since the power of nation states is built on the idea of sovereignty over territory. How that territory is held, who owns it and what role they play in society is of vital concern.

Historically, the integrity of nation states was secured by an intimate relationship between the monarch and the aristocracy. This relationship is most vividly illustrated by the ideas of feudalism by which states managed to consolidate political power through a powerful system of patronage involving feudal grants of their territory. As states became more stable and this relationship weakened (elites became more powerful and the Crown less so), so land became more and more of an economic power base, and landowners made strenuous efforts to consolidate their ownership and loosen conditions which bound them to the Crown.

Today, from South Africa to Zimbabwe, from Brazil to Hungary, and from Canada to Australia, disputes about the ownership and distribution of land continue to

create tension and political struggles. Not surprisingly,
much of the debate about land comes down to questions
of power and control. Land is political.

The Environmental Discourse

In recent decades environmental concerns have climbed
up the political agenda. Issues ranging from global
warming to deforestation and from soil erosion to
biodiversity are influenced by how people manage the
environment. As Aldo Leopold the American human
ecologist observed:

'Conservation is getting nowhere because it is
incompatible with our Abrahamic concept of land. We
abuse land because we regard it as a commodity belonging
to us. When we see land as a community to which we
belong, we may begin to use it with love and respect.'[8]

Statutory regulation and law can play a part in arresting
environmental destruction and degradation, and
environmental law is now an important area of law in
itself. But as the job of conserving and protecting the
environment gets ever more challenging, it is becoming
clear that nothing less than a revolution in our relationship with the earth is required to bring about change.

And it is impossible to talk about changing this
relationship without at some time confronting the legal
reality that every flower, tree and hedgerow forms part
of land and is thus legally owned. Attempts to reform
behaviour through the imposition of statute law can
only have a limited, localised, and short-term effect.
They fail most dramatically when faced with certain
power structures, foremost among which is the
ownership of land and the framework of land tenure
which defines and governs the relationship between a
society and its territory.

The ownership of land confers rights on individuals in
society. Environmental stewardship demands that those

rights should be accompanied by responsibilities to the rest of society and, ultimately, to the planet. This reciprocal relationship has yet to be acknowledged legally in land tenure systems.

Theology

Leopold's reference to Abraham underlines the profound influence that theology has had on modern attitudes to land and the sensitive question of its ownership and control. This is even more pronounced in a Scottish context because of our history and because under feudal tenure Scotland is owned in the final analysis not by landowners, not by the Crown, but by God.

And if such an appeal to theology appears irrelevant at the cusp of a new and secular millennium, theologian Alastair McIntosh argues that like it or not, such is the law of the land. 'Under Scots feudal law God is the ultimate owner of the land and all others are vassals unto the Lord.'[9] Land law in Scotland is thus theocratic and, as Alastair points out, the authoritative Anchor Bible Dictionary states that, 'the land theme is so ubiquitous that it may have greater claim to be the central motif in the Old Testament than any other, including covenant'. Some understanding of what God means is not just of academic or theological relevance but of real legal note, as demonstrated recently by McIntosh's expert advice for the defence in a case involving the eviction of a tenant of a holiday hut on the Carbeth Estate north of Glasgow.

And indeed the Old Testament, which has much to say on the land question, played an important part in the land agitations in the 17th, 18th and 19th centuries and was the authority cited by the Diggers, Levellers, and the Highland Land League in their efforts for a more just division of land and access to resources.[10] Paradoxically, landed power has also proved a particularly contentious issue within the Church of Scotland given the history of landed patronage and the central role played by that concept in the Disruption of 1843.

More recently, theologians such as Professor Donald MacLeod of the Free Church College have articulated a theologically derived radical agenda for land reform. 'We are slaves of the past', he writes, 'oppressed by title deeds which do no more than give a veneer of legality to the whims of ancient monarchs, the crimes of mediaeval brigands and the insufferable vanity of Highland chiefs. The campaign for land reform is driven by ideals; by a desire to curtail the powerful and to empower the disempowered; by a concern for stewardship and community; by a passion for freedom and justice.'[11]

Land Reform in Scotland Today

The arguments and approaches outlined above all have something important to say about why land reform is important and how it can bring economic, social and environmental benefits by beginning to change for good the pattern and legacy of the past. The Scottish Land Reform Convention, an independent civic forum set up by the Convention of Scottish Local Authorities (COSLA), the Scottish Trades Union Congress (STUC), Action of Churches Together in Scotland (ACTS) and the Scottish Council for Voluntary Organisations (SCVO) to promote debate and action on land reform, has adopted sovereignty, democracy, social justice and stewardship as its four guiding principles. These are based on the premise that the land of Scotland is held by the people of Scotland as the ultimate sovereign authority, that decisions as to how it should be owned and used are to be determined through the democratic process of the Scots Parliament, and that social justice and stewardship are two fundamental goals of land reform.

So what exactly is land reform? Is it a question of reining in the worst excesses and providing some palliative relief in acute circumstances, or is it a question of reforming the structures and processes which have driven us inexorably to the current system of tenure and division of land? To what extent does the term cover the range of diverse subjects related to land from feudal tenure to how we regulate the use of the sea, from the structure of farming to good relations in a tenement, from the management of wild game to the provision of affordable housing, and from conserving nature to local democracy?

Such a wide-ranging set of issues raises an important point. Current land reform proposals embrace a huge range of topics from feudal reform to access rights, from national parks to landlord-tenant relations.[12] Much of this wider agenda is not strictly-speaking land reform but land policy, i.e. government or public policy towards how land is used and managed. Land reform, on the other hand, is about the nature and distribution of power over land and is quite distinct from how that power is then exercised, i.e. how land is then used.

Land reform is about reforming power structures, social relationships, and modes of production. It has certain core values of equity, social justice, democracy and environmental stewardship. There is a public interest in all land and there are choices to be made: choices between the free market and a social market, between land accumulation and land redistribution, between paternalism and empowerment, between Scotland for the people and Scotland for everyone but the people.

This is where the idea of redistributing power comes in. Sensitive to charges of seeking to promote land nationalisation, politicians who believe in land reform have been careful not to use the term land redistribution. But the redistribution of power is not the same as the redistribution of land even although it may, in the end, lead to similar outcomes.

Redistributing land suggests a centralised process of expropriation and redistribution, an idea whose time has gone. But redistributing power over land is about checking the stranglehold of landed power, and about allowing many more people in society to have a responsible say in how land is owned, how it is divided, who owns it, how much they own, how it is used and managed – and to enjoy a share of the benefits which flow from sound land use.

In the light of this view of how land reform should be prosecuted, how has the debate been framed politically in recent years?

REFERENCES

1. Rousseau, 1754.
2. MacGregor, 1993, pp. 10–11.
3. Stiefel & Wolfe, 1994, p. 40–70.
4. Hunter, 1998, p. 36.
5. Marx, Capital. pp. 875–876.
6. Harrison, *Losses of Nations*. pp. 42–43, p. 46, pp. 113–116.
7. Timperley, *The Pattern of Landholding in Eighteenth-Century Scotland*, p. 137.
8. Leopold, *Sand County Almanac*, p. xviii.
9. McIntosh, 1999.
10. Meek, 1987 and Hill, 1991.
11. MacLeod, 1998.
12. Scottish Office, 1999.

Chapter 4
The Politics of Land Reform

The enemy is the landlord, the agent, the capitalist, and the Parliament which makes and maintains iniquitous laws. Cut down the telegraph wires and posts, carry away the wires and the instruments! Stop the mail-carts, destroy the letters, etc... Burn the property of all obnoxious landlords, agents etc. Set fire to the heather to destroy the game; disturb the deer; poison game dogs! The oppressed toilers of England and the millions of disinherited people are watching your actions. Their hearts are with you in your battle for right and liberty.
'God Save the People!'

LAND RESTORATION LEAGUE MANIFESTO

The politics of land reform are a far cry from the sentiments expressed above at the height of the land agitation in the late 19th century and, in terms of its appeal to violence, this is certainly welcome. But perhaps, in the process, something of the spirit of social justice which impelled the land reformers of last century has been lost. For today, despite all the heady rhetoric, there appears to be little appetite for radical reform.

This is not only because modern politics has lost the reforming zeal of the past but because any land reform which entertains a fundamental shift in power faces formidable obstacles which have built up over the years. These obstacles are legal, political and financial. Property rights are a fiercely defended institution and in a post-modern, post-industrial world it is easy to pretend that land does not matter any more (at least beyond the concerns of a few crofters and communities in the Highlands). Sure, there is a case for some modernisation of the law, some better protection and help for fragile areas but beyond that is there a problem?

The absence of a legislature in Scotland has been one of the key reasons why the land question has not been addressed for so long. It was a measure of the seriousness with which Gladstone took agitation in the Highlands that the British Government passed crofting laws. Only when faced with the serious prospect of political unrest has Westminster sat up and done anything. Inevitably such responses have represented something of a palliative to the real problems. Crofters, for example, did not just want security of tenure on the miserable bits of ground they had been pushed onto – they wanted back the land from which they had been evicted.

Whenever the land question has come to the fore in political debate, party allegiances and traditions have been resurrected, prejudices reinforced and the half-forgotten rhetoric of history has been given an airing in one of the few areas where it can still safely be deployed. For much of the 20th century, political debate was never going to change anything and politicians could indulge in rhetorical flourishes without having to face up to the consequences of their oratory.

Those on the left of the political spectrum have traditionally taken up positions ranging from outright nationalisation to penal taxes as ways of challenging landed power. The right has continued in its role as defender of private property and the existing division of land, instinctively regarding any measure to interfere with them as tantamount to revolution. Such instincts even led Michael Forsyth to react with horror when it was proposed that a new streamlined method of gaining access to existing datasets about land being developed by the Royal Incorporation of Chartered Surveyors should include improvements in access to property ownership information. He needed a gentle reminder from civil servants that such details have been publicly available in the Register of Sasines since 1617!

The new politics in Scotland and the opportunities it provides for tackling the problem has given politicians a challenge. Thinking on the topic has never been very deep and more often than not, outrage and bluster have been the sole currency of debate. Even during the long years of Tory rule in the 1980s and 1990s campaigning newspapers such as the *West Highland Free Press*, the leading organ of the left in a region where land reform is topical and which has played a vital role in elevating the subject to its rightful place, never actually managed to develop a coherent political agenda for change.

Neither, it should be said, did any of the political parties. And so, as they now come to terms with a debate which is highly political, they are somewhat disorientated and seem reluctant to follow their instincts, perhaps through anxiety over whether political ideology has a part to play in land reform. The centre ground of politics is so crowded that such a fundamental axiom – 'land is power' – appears to be forgotten, even denied. Even so, some semblance of political philosophy can be detected in the main political parties.

The Conservatives have traditionally been the party to which landowning interests, most intuitively attach themselves. That fusion was strained by the Thatcher years when a new, more radical right wing agenda, which sought to capture individualistic aspirations across the social classes, marginalised the patrician landed Tory. But in one important ideological sense the Tories under Thatcher (and since) have set out a new vision of land and property – an ideological crusade to promote home ownership. This mainly took the form of encouraging mortgage lending and, controversially, giving council house tenants the right to buy.

This policy was remarkably successful. In extending home ownership, the political right was creating a new expanded 'property-owning democracy' which could be

relied on (or so it thought) to vote Conservative. What
was inconsistent about this ideology, however, was that
it limited the ideals of property ownership to the home.
There was no promotion of a property-owning
democracy in the countryside – precisely the opposite, in
fact. Tory cabinets were stuffed with apologists for the
landed classes, who would have as soon countenanced
an extension of a property-owning democracy in rural
Perthshire as they would have engaged in a massive
programme of nationalisation of heavy industry.

Despite taking on and defeating much of the British
Establishment, Thatcher and her disciples remained
curiously in awe of landed power. This is surprising
since, as James Hunter recently observed: 'land reform,
though often advocated in advance of its occurrence by
the left, almost always ends, when it is actually put into
practice, by greatly strengthening the right'[1] – because it
creates a very large class of small-scale owner-occupiers.

Labour, on the other hand, has remained burdened with
the legacy of state socialism and state ownership. The left,
perhaps in reaction to the excesses of Victorian and
Edwardian capitalism, has sought refuge in the power of
the state to solve economic and social problems. Two
centuries of landed power had smashed the peasantry,
and thus the potential engine for an alternative socialist
model based upon co-operatives of small scale proprietors
controlling the land and economy was denied – this,
despite the efforts of the Chartists and others in the 19th
century and of the early leaders of the Labour Party
whose municipal socialism in urban areas yielded great
advances in many parts of urban Scotland.[2]

A third way – a social democratic property-owning
society with strong mutual and co-operative institutions
– the way of Scandinavia and much of western Europe –
was denied Britain not only by the weakness of the
peasantry but also by the collapse of the Liberals and

the rejection of the co-operative, social economy model by the Left in Britain in favour of state ownership.

Curiously, given their history, it is the Liberals who display least certainty, commitment or passion about land reform, even though their political traditions and many individual Liberals have much to offer. The other party in Scottish politics, the SNP, has traditionally adopted a high profile on the land question but, like Labour, has tended to promote a diffuse political philosophy which shies away from contentious political issues. Their recent Scottish Land Commission barely touched the subject of landownership, although the ostensible objective of the Commission was 'to consider land use in Scotland and to recommend how this important resource can be used for the benefit of the Scottish People as a whole.'[3] Quite how it is possible to conduct such an enquiry and ignore the scandalous pattern of landownership remains something of a mystery although some party sources suggest the issue has been dodged deliberately to deflect controversy.

Both the Green Party and Scottish Socialist Party are now represented in the new Parliament. This will hopefully result in a more radical perspective on land reform emerging within mainstream party political debate. Aside from political parties, however, the debate about land reform has been influenced by several other important discourses and value systems. Perhaps it is only proper to start with the landowners themselves.

The Landed Interest

The institution of landownership, as has been argued, has provided a extraordinary bastion of power and privilege which has deterred any serious attempt at dismantling. The landed interest might appear to be modest in number but it remains formidable in its influence. As the late Margaret MacPherson observed, 'it would be as easy to pare the claws of a tiger running loose in the jungle as control the laird with his factor, accountants, lawyers, friends in the Scottish Landowners' Federation and the House of Lords.'[4]

The strength of the institution is also its greatest weakness since it has very few members and, as the debate develops, it is going to have to acknowledge this weakness since one powerful argument for land reform is that it can dramatically increase the number of landowners. Such a perspective is routinely dismissed by landed interests, even though it could be their route to far greater political clout in the politics of the new Scotland.

The Scottish Landowners' Federation (SLF), which represents around 3,000 landowners who are in possession of around 40 per cent of private rural land in Scotland,[5] has been shaken from its slumbers by the Government's land reform plans and by the existence of the Scottish Parliament, within which neither they nor their friends in the Tory party can envisage having much influence.

The response of the landed establishment to the prospect of land reform is revealing. Much of it has been complacent, naive, unsophisticated, reactionary, amateurish and confused. Lacking any grasp of the issue, why it has sprung to prominence, or how to respond to it, huddles of inarticulate, bemused lairds have been gathering together in meetings to try and make sense of a political landscape changed out of all recognition from the cosy, well ordered and predictable world they knew before. And in a litany of invective, hypocrisy and cant the lackeys of the

huddles of inarticulate, bemused lairds have been gathering together in meetings to try and make sense of a political landscape changed out of all recognition from the cosy, well ordered and predictable world they knew before.

landowners – the lawyers, accountants and land agents (who often have the most to lose), denounce land reform proposals. In the process they display the visceral prejudices of the propertied and monied classes which have become ingrained deep within their psyche.

Those who stand to gain from land reform, particularly crofters, local communities, and walkers – are disparagingly dismissed as feckless, undeserving, and incompetent. 'Look at crofters,' some members of the landed classes claim, '40 per cent of crofts are unworked or underworked'. As for local communities, 'what do they know about how to manage land, what conditions are going to be placed on public money given in support of community buyouts?' And walkers? Well, 'who's going to police them, what about litter, and who's going to pay the inevitable costs that will arise from a freedom to roam?'[6] In displaying such prejudice they do all of us a service by clarifying the real agenda of landed interests – to discredit land reform in order to protect landed power and privilege.

They will, however, fail in this course of action since for every argument they deploy they expose their own feeble case. Community groups should be assessed for competence, they argue, and there should be clawback of public funds if their venture fails. They should present a business plan before they can be given the right to purchase land. Oh yes? So what about other landowners. Do they have to be assessed for competence, will they hand back all the tax breaks and subsidies if their business fails, will they accept a host of conditions on the public money they receive, will other prospective purchasers of Scottish real estate present business plans in advance?

The more intelligent, progressive and smart landowners and agents, however, are being rather more circumspect in their approach, realising perhaps that keeping quiet and

Don't lecture me laddie about caring for the hills and and the long walk in! So what if you've walked 20 miles for your wilderness experience – we've paid £500 for our sport here so piss off!

keeping their heads down is a strategy which has served them well in the past. The rhetorical zeal for land reform, it is assumed, will fizzle out once the Parliament encounters the formidable difficulties associated with reform. Worryingly, of course, this may indeed be the case!

Whatever strategy proves the more successful, it is unlikely to be possible to put the genie back in the bottle. Land reform is now mainstream and is attracting support from some unlikely quarters in the Scottish Establishment. Whatever legislative programme is embarked upon by the Parliament, there will be a growing level of scrutiny, analysis and debate which will improve with time and which will deepen and broaden people's understanding of the real nature of the land problem. Landed interests are faced with a choice. They can go with the flow or they can resist. Never before has the importance of making the right choice been so acute.

And here it is interesting to note the reaction of lairds like the Duke of Buccleuch, who has made it clear he would be happy to see a mechanism for getting rid of 'bad landowners'.[7] In other words, landed interests are prepared to see government intervention where it suits their purposes (eliminating the kinds of people who not only cause so much misery but in the process do much to harm the interests of other Scottish landowners) but not where it doesn't.

On the broader front, the SLF appears to have adopted a strategy of damage limitation. Keep land reform restricted to the far north and west, to crofters and to communities in places like Knoydart and leave the rest of us in peace. It is a strategy similar to that adopted in 1880s when unrest among crofters was addressed by restricting any reform to the parts of Scotland which posed least threat to landowning interests.

It is not only landed interests who are struggling to get to grips with an agenda which at times appears very simple (the Eigg & Knoydart syndrome) and at other times appears far more complex (the details of property law, planning, land value and taxation). Politicians, academics, journalists, lawyers and indeed most of the rest of us are also poorly equipped to engage in a debate which for so long has been denied and forbidden.

In particular, the debate which is now well underway is in danger of being confused by two discourses which have emerged in recent years. The first concerns the idea that proposals to be implemented by the Scottish Executive are radical. The second is an impression which has been created that land reform is a Highland issue.

A Radical Agenda

It is difficult to judge how radical current proposals[8] really are. Not only is any action on land reform relatively radical but the basis on which it can be judged varies. Are the proposals launched by the Scottish Office in January 1999 – and which the Scottish Executive has said it will enact – radical?

Whilst leading landowners claimed they were relaxed about the proposals, some politicians claimed that they met all the expectations of land reformers built up over the years. Can they both be right? Well probably they can, because land reform which does something to deal with worst cases can be portrayed as radical since that is what people have been told the problem involves (Eigg & Knoydart). Many landowners can relax because nothing is being proposed which interferes with their affairs (particularly if they are 'good landowners' who have, according to Government, nothing to fear from reform). The fact that so-called 'bad' landowners have nothing to fear either rather undermines the rhetoric!

On the other hand, if one were to believe Government spin doctors, lairds have everything to fear.

The headline in *Scotland on Sunday* on 3 January 1999 screamed:

Rogue Lairds to have their land sold off
Abolition of the feudal system a radical move against abuses by absentee owners

'Absentee lairds', it reported, 'who mismanage their estates will be forced to sell their land to the state under radical new plans to be announced this week.'

It was a classic piece of spin designed to fortify the 'radical nature' of the Land Reform Policy Group proposals which were to be launched two days later. It provoked outrage from landowners. 'This idea sparks feelings of absolute horror in me. It is a recipe for total disaster', fulminated Graeme Gordon, ex-Convenor of SLF.[9] After all the fuss had died down and the plans became public, however, it became clear that no such powers were proposed and landowners were assured that they had nothing to fear from the plans. But by now the spin had produced the desired results among the general public.

No matter that there were no plans to punish rogue lairds and no matter that nothing would be done about absentee landowners (good or bad). No matter either that the abolition of feudalism has absolutely nothing to do with either bad lairds, abuses of ownership or absenteeism! *The Scotsman* of 25 January 1999 reported that Prince Abdul Aziz al-Thani, a member of the ruling family of the Gulf state of Qatar, had bought the Newmiln Estate in Perthshire for £2.3 million. According to the report, this gentleman will now be subject to the Government's proposals to check-up on absentee landlords in Scotland and faces having his land seized if he mismanages it. Prince Abdul, of course, need not worry about anything of the sort and can enjoy his new estate in peace.

And the rhetoric goes on. Brian Wilson MP, speaking

Don't worry Sir Ogilvie-Brodie-Pratt, good landowners have nothing to fear from the Scottish Executive's land reform proposals (and, by the way, neither do bad ones).

about the Uig area on Lewis, talked of 'the dead hand
and petty tyrannies of absentee private landlordism.'[10]
Tyranny certainly, and a state of affairs which can be
overcome by proposals which will give crofters in Uig
the right to take ownership of their common grazings.
Outside of the crofting areas, however, there is nothing
to stop that state of affairs continuing indefinitely, since
Government plans explicitly reject any moves to tackle
absentee landlordism (tyrannical or otherwise).

Which all suggests that the politics of land reform, as
Dr Ewen Cameron, a Highland historian at Edinburgh
University, recently observed, 'represent the pursuit of
what is least disruptive, the minimum possible reform to
retain support and to argue that promises have been
fulfilled whilst alienating the fewest.'[11]

Which is not to say that what has been proposed to date
is meaningless. Far from it – it is a useful start which
will deliver welcome change. But it is not as radical as
reforming politicians would have us believe.

The Highlandification of Land Reform
Finally, the land question in the Highlands has a
particular resonance and meaning for good historical
reasons. The prominent coverage given to events in
Assynt, Eigg and Knoydart have managed to create the
impression that land reform is therefore an issue for the
Highlands alone. This perception led Donald Dewar to
make a telling comment recently:

'... the land document (the final report of the Scottish
Office Land Reform Policy Group) was radical... it was
greeted throughout the Highlands with immense
satisfaction and very strong support.'[12]

One of the problems in Scottish politics is that there are
few politicians who are genuinely interested or
knowledgeable about land reform or who have a track
record of engagement with it. The few that are (Brian
Wilson, Calum Macdonald, and Roseanna Cunningham

among others) care passionately. But for most others the land issue is something which it is convenient to acknowledge rather than understand. The media has therefore become massively influential in creating what little awareness and knowledge there is about the topic and has, perhaps unwittingly, fostered the view that land reform is a Highland issue and something only to do with crofters.

Such a perception exposes the alarming immaturity of the debate. To frame the debate as a Highland issue reinforces the stereotypical view generated by the media and allows politicians to contain the issue in a part of the country where it can safely be handled.

The Scottish Parliament will indeed provide the time, and hopefully the political will, to tackle land reform. But powerful networks of vested interests will have the time and the money to ensure that the more radical reforms are either diluted or abandoned. If the boat is not pushed out now, the land question may again become a little local difficulty among crofters and locals in the far flung periphery of the north and west Highlands. The landowning power bloc has historically been keen to promote the notion of a little local difficulty in the North and it suits their interests very well to see that happen again.

If the boat is not pushed out now, the land question may again become a little local difficulty among crofters and locals in the far flung periphery of the north and west Highlands.

The chance does not come often to have fundamental reform of ancient and deeply embedded land laws and structures. So what exactly do the measures now being promoted by the Scottish Executive seek to do and will they work?

REFERENCES

1. Hunter, 1995.
2. Tom Johnston's *A History of the Working Classes in Scotland* is illuminating on this in his chapter 'The Communist Seeds of Salvation'.
3. Scottish Land Commission, 1997.
4. MacPherson in: Evans & Hendry, 1985, p. 20.
5. Wightman, 1996b, p. 153.
6. Much of this kind of attitude was on display at a conference, 'Land Reform in Real Life' organised by Turcan Connell Solicitors and Saffrey Champness Chartered Accountants held in Edinburgh, 24 February 1999. Proceedings are available from the organisers.
7. 'Laird of 270,000 acres warns over false Utopias'. *The Guardian*, 6 January 1999, p. 3
8. Scottish Office, 1999. These form the basis of the Labour/Lib Dem partnership programme for government. (*Partnership for Scotland – An Agreement for the first Scottish Parliament*, May 1999). 'We will... legislate on the proposals of the Land Reform Group.'
9. *Scotland on Sunday*, 3 January 1999.
10. *West Highland Free Press*, 5 March 1999.
11. Cameron, 1998.
12. 'The Scotsman Debate'. *The Scotsman*, 5 February 1999 p. v.

Chapter 5
A Critique of Existing Proposals

Land reform is now no longer a fringe concern. There is a substantial political consensus for action. On 14 May 1999 Donald Dewar and Jim Wallace signed the 'Partnership for Scotland' which forms the basis for the Government of Scotland for the next four years.[1] In it, they commit themselves to the abolition of feudal tenure and to implementing the proposals of the Land Reform Policy Group (LRPG), set up by the Scottish Office in 1997, and whose final report, *Recommendations for Action*[2] was launched in January 1999. The Liberal Democrats' manifesto commitments to provide a right to buy for agricultural tenants, to enhance local councils' powers of compulsory purchase, to establish a Standing Commission on landownership, and to establish a land bank were all ditched.

What is to be made of the LRPG agenda for land reform? Is it well-informed, well targeted, and radical? To listen to the politicians one might think so. But on closer examination, much of it turns out to be shallow and superficial, presenting a range of palliative measures which address symptoms rather than underlying problems. And it is the core proposal for land reform, namely the much vaunted community right-to-buy, which is most fundamentally flawed. Before looking at that, however, what of the policy that all would-be land reforming politicians have been keen to embrace, the abolition of feudalism?

The Abolition of Feudalism
Much was made of the sovereignty of the Scottish people on the day our new Parliamentarians took their oath in the Assembly Hall on the Mound on Wednesday 12 May 1999. The Claim of Right, signed by Scotland's politicians, was invoked as the underpinning of Scotland's new democracy and rightly so. Ironically,

however, Parliament will soon get down to work on the abolition of feudalism, which will involve, as proposals stand currently, the denial and elimination of the most profound expression of that same sovereignty.

All land in Scotland is held under the sovereign authority of the Crown and of Parliament. In addition, the Crown, as Paramount Superior, retains a direct proprietorial interest in those parts of Scotland held in feudal tenure. Thus under the same doctrine expounded in the Claim of Right, we the people are the ultimate owners of Scotland. Embedded in this relationship is the concept of conditionality – the historic reality that power over land has always been divided and that landowners have always been constrained in the exercise of property rights by the will of Parliament and by the conditions in their titles.

But (and this is the irony in the situation), the current proposals of the Scottish Executive involve the scrapping of the Crown as Paramount Superior. This conditionality is to be jettisoned, the landowner is to be made King or Queen and the absolute owner of his or her land – a concept alien to almost 900 years of Scottish legal theory. Scotland, in one of the first acts of our new Parliament, is to be given away to those who in many cases have inherited their interest from the ancient theft of the land many centuries ago.

It is little surprise that members of the Scottish Landowners' Federation are among the most enthusiastic advocates of the abolition of the last vestiges of the feudal system. At a stroke the public interest in feudal Scotland is eliminated with the stigma of feudalism removed, and a powerful symbolic stick in the land reformer's lexicon is destroyed.

Of further note is the fact that the abolition of feudalism, the focus of so much political rhetoric, is so underwhelming in its impact on the division of land in

*The abolition of feudalism and the landowner is made King.
Scotland, in one of the first acts of our new Parliament, is to be
given away – the defiant and ultimate triumph of a project begun
around 800 years ago by the Scottish aristocracy to wrest to
themselves all power over land from the Crown.*

Scotland. The abandonment of this system after 900 years will have no impact on the concentrated pattern of landownership in Scotland and will in fact strengthen the position of landowners. Whilst the abolition of feudalism is a desirable thing for small-scale homeowners, it will do nothing to alter the basic power structures in the countryside.

We will wake up the day after the feudal reform act is passed into law and nothing substantial will have changed. Indeed, had the act emanated from the previous Scots Parliament almost 300 years ago, the sorry history of those centuries would have been much the same despite the claim by one leading politician recently that feudal abolition would have prevented the Highland Clearances! Why? The Clearances were made possible not so much by feudal tenure as by the laws of succession to land, the unregulated market in land, the insecurity of tenants, the concentrated pattern of landownership and the nature of the rights that go with property. None of these factors is being tackled by the current proposals for land reform.

We will wake up the day after the feudal reform act is passed into law and nothing substantial will have changed.

It is of supreme concern that we are about to initiate legislation which, under the popular guise of land reform will, if handled as planned, be the defiant and ultimate triumph of a project begun around 800 years ago by the Scottish aristocracy, namely to wrest to themselves all power over land from the Crown. They have been remarkably successful so far because they have made the land laws of this country. What an unbelievable irony if, just as the House of Lords in the Palace of Westminster loses the power to revise Scottish legislation, a land reforming Scottish Executive delivers to the lairds their final prize in its first piece of legislation!

The Fashionable Idea of Community

Community ownership is the centrepiece of the Scottish Executive's proposals for land reform. The White Paper launched by Jim Wallace on 8 July 1999 spells out the details of how this power is to be framed.[3] No one, it appears, can aspire to be in the vanguard of land reform if they don't pay homage to this holy grail of land reform. It has become to the 1990s debate on the subject what nationalisation was to the debate in the 1970s.

As one critic has observed, 'concepts such as community involvement, participation, and empowerment are not a particularly new set of ideas. They have been trucked around the developing world for the last 30 odd years by experts in the World Bank and United Nations agencies with little real success. This muddled thinking on community has now entered the minds of the wise persons who title themselves the Land Reform Policy Group. However, in hitching themselves to the community of place banner they have done so with little research, knowledge or understanding of the social land movement and its 150 years of organised effort. Such an opportunistic, narrow and exclusive approach to social landownership is not good enough nor strategic enough to enable Scotland-wide policy to be developed'.

Moreover, 'Government and public agencies have seized on ideas of community, community development, inclusion and empowerment. But the institutions of Government are not particularly participatory, inclusive or empowering and this agenda is driven from above, through centralised agencies and distant bureaucracies which operate to narrow Ministerial directives and managerial instructions that are locked firmly in the grip of the civil service administration and its rules and regulations. We have institutionalised participation in which the State decides and determines the policies and permitted actions and the terms of reference for them.'[4]

The problem with the White Paper's approach is that it promotes community ownership and community involvement as solutions to the problems inherent in the existing system. Let's look at community ownership first.

Community Ownership

In the widely-publicised cases of Eigg and Knoydart, the concerns of the community were focused on an uncertain future in which anyone from anywhere could buy the whole estate. The factors which led to the situation in which Eigg and Knoydart found themselves were:

- an unregulated market in land
- the scale of the holding on offer (together with the Edwardian and Victorian infrastructure)
- the lack of obligations on any prospective purchaser.

It was against this background that the communities concerned decided that the way forward lay in taking the estates into community ownership, in partnership with others. That was the appropriate response in a situation where they were powerless to do anything else. Communities bought the land because of the failure of the system to provide anything other than an international speculator's lottery.

Proposals to entrench the community right-to-buy as a legislative right when land comes up for sale may provide the right solution in some circumstances, but they do implicitly treat the symptoms of the problem rather than the circumstances which brought the situation about. If such large estates as Eigg and Knoydart did not exist, if those who owned them were many in number and were resident, working individuals and families, the problem would never have arisen in the first place.

In other words, if measures are taken to secure a smaller-scale pattern of landownership involving

Welcome to Auchenshoogle village hall. I'm pleased to report that Scottish Ministers have accepted and registered our interest in the land on Muckle Estate. All we have to do now is wait for it to come onto the market so go home and tell your great-great-great-grandchildren to prepare to exercise their right-to-buy!

resident landowners in a market which is regulated (even modestly), then the kinds of crisis which paralysed Eigg and Knoydart for so many years would never have emerged.

The community right-to-buy is a proposal born out of an acceptance of the current division of land and the unregulated market. It is a proposal whose application demands a lot of communities dissatisfied with the status quo. It is a measure which treats the symptoms of the problem rather than its underlying causes. And it is a measure which will, in any event, only be available in the most restricted of circumstances:

- where the community has previously set up a trust and registered an interest in land
- when the property comes onto the market
- where the trust then votes to pursue ownership
- if they can raise the funds.

In terms of just one of these conditions (land which comes on the market), the mechanism is likely to be available in a tiny number of instances.

Over the years 1990 to 1998, around 250 farms, 20 estates and 30 forest properties were sold each year. Given that there is no evidence of communities wishing to buy farms, the availability is restricted to around 20 estates and 30 forest properties. A casual look at most of these reveals a limited appeal to communities since they consist in the main of sporting estates and Sitka spruce plantations. Land which is likely to be of appeal will be determined by the communities themselves, but its availability will be determined by the owner.

Most private land in Scotland has never been exposed for sale (privately or openly) for over 100 years. It is estimated, for example, that at least 25 per cent of estates of over 1,000 acres in Scotland have been held by the same families for over 400 years.[5] Even in parts of Scotland where turnover is higher such as the Highlands, over 50 per cent of private land has never been exposed since the war and 25 per cent has not been exposed at any time in the 20th century. The community right-to-buy might better be described as a right-to-buy for the great-grandchildren of the community!

Most private land in Scotland has never been exposed for sale (privately or openly) for over 100 years.

Government claims that a community right-to-buy would 'greatly empower communities' and 'effect rapid change in the pattern of landownership'[6] are therefore plain nonsense. No community is going to be empowered through speculation that at some point in the future, they might be able to take over control of the land. There will be no rapid change in the pattern of landownership – that will remain largely unaffected by these proposals. Given that these are the *only two advantages* cited by the LRPG report it is hard to see the justification for pursuing this option with any determination.

Moreover, it is worth noting that the purchase of both Eigg and Knoydart were achieved as a result of:

- negotiations with creditors (which reduced the asking price by 30-50 per cent)
- availability of generous donations from benefactors
- large sums of money raised through the voluntary conservation movement
- long and sustained exposure in the media which galvanised interested parties
- a landowner whose image was poor and thus helpful in attracting sympathetic media coverage of the community's plight.

These circumstances will not always apply. Purchases (notwithstanding the intervention of a government appointed valuer) will have to be negotiated within tight time-frames, based on higher prices, with progressively less public generosity, and in circumstances where the seller is not a villain.

It is invidious to put communities in an either/or situation: either buy land or face a fate determined by the open market. The danger is that communities will feel pressured into going for community ownership as the only course of action available to them. A decision not to go ahead will be met with mutterings that 'oh well they had their chance'. In a politically charged atmosphere it seems rather unfair and disingenuous to put such a burden on communities.

The former Scottish Office Minister Lord Sewel claimed recently (re Knoydart):

'At the end of the day I come down very firmly on the side of local community-led development. Clearly, well-run estates operate in a way that facilitates local community development. The problems arise, and the challenges arise when the way in which an estate is managed does not allow the local community to develop economically and socially.'[7]

Recognising that estates can be run in ways which do not allow the local community to develop economically and socially is to recognise that estates themselves are the problem. Landholdings that are of such a scale as to even be in a position to influence the economic and social development of communities are bad news.

No community can develop its full potential when decision-making is in the hands of the owners of local estates, no matter how well run the estates might appear to be. Development is about liberating and empowering people. Arguing that well-run estates do this is Victorian paternalistic cant. Massive landholdings concentrate power in a few hands and almost inevitably determine the mode of production in the locality. They are disabling and disempowering. Such a situation is not only socially unjust, it is often a recipe for economic failure.

There is a further problem with the promotion of community ownership. In many cases there is a broad community interest in how land is owned and used, but the vehicle for taking this interest forward is not necessarily community ownership. Community development thinking suggests that it is the provision of a diversity of opportunities that delivers the most sustainable solutions. In other words, there should be opportunities both for individuals and for groups within communities to access land, together with possibilities of partnership with national voluntary organisations, as happened in the cases of both Eigg and Knoydart. Indeed there should also be opportunities for the wider social landownership movement operating through co-operative, mutual and national voluntary organisations to break into the land market more effectively on its own account.

Now all of this may appear to represent a fairly downbeat assessment of the Scottish Executive's flagship land reform proposal. But a proposal which ignores the fundamental causes of the situations it seeks to resolve may end up creating more misery by forcing communities to choose between the uncertainties of the market and the uncertainties of community ownership. The unregulated market in huge swathes of territory organised in the form of outdated estates is the underlying cause of the crisis in many of the more fragile communities in Scotland.

In order to attract investment, and to provide security, diversity and prosperity, land reform should be aiming to break up large holdings to enable people to purchase property within a regulated framework which insists on residency and limits monopoly holdings. No community should find itself at the mercy of one landowner whose actions (or inactions) affect the entire locality. A small-scale pattern of landownership disperses power, creates less potential for abuse (which if it does occur is over a much smaller area and impacts on far fewer people), and less scope for disinterest and apathy. In short, more landowners means more diversity, more investment, more opportunities, and more accountability.

Before developing such proposals further, let's consider the other fashionable land reform cause – community involvement.

Community Involvement
Much land reform rhetoric has centred around the idea of 'increased community involvement in the way land is owned and used.'[8] Community involvement in the way land is owned would involve local communities in determining the nature and pattern of local landownership – a radical and useful idea but, unfortunately, mere rhetoric. There are no proposals from any political party to implement such an idea – precisely the opposite in fact.

Community involvement in how land is used has some more substance in the Scottish Executive's proposals and the SNP are keen on community contracts with landowners and Locality Land Councils. But this all begs some fundamental questions about who is to be involved in whose land, to what degree, when and with what authority, powers, responsibility and resources. It also begs some matters of principle.

The basic understanding of property rights within the Scots law of property rests on the notion that landowners are entitled to use their property as they wish, subject to their title and any statutory constraints.

Furthermore, the European Convention on Human Rights protects the rights of landowners to the 'peaceful enjoyment' of their possessions. On this basis it seems a rather dramatic move to promote the idea of the community being involved in the use and management of private property.

Of course at a certain level the community is already involved through the statutory provisions of, for example, the planning system. But community involvement as it is promoted argues for local involvement in the plans and ideas for the use and management of specific parcels of private property. Whilst this may be taken forward on a voluntary basis within the law it is harder to see how it can be legislated for without infringing the rights of property – which leads to the matter of principle. Is it right, proper or just in a liberal democracy for individuals to involve themselves in the internal affairs of property owners?

If landowners are to be entitled to enjoy certain private rights (together with responsibilities), should not part of this be the freedom to enjoy the use of property free from interference by others? Is it seriously being suggested that homeowners and farmers be obliged to consult and adhere to the views and opinions of others in the community, to consult on matters to do with how the vegetable plot should be laid out or what crops to grow next year?

The answer is an emphatic no. What is clear is that such involvement is to be restricted in scope to the affairs of large landowners with community involvement in the use and management of large estates. What such a proposal really reflects is the inordinate power that the property system affords those who own large areas of land. The problem is not the property system nor indeed disempowered communities, but large-scale holdings.

If there are to be thresholds for such involvement it will

be relatively straightforward to restructure holdings so as to escape scrutiny. Such an arrangement also offends the principle of privacy and citizen's rights that we would be anxious to afford homeowners and farmers. It introduces a differential system of property rights which is not only questionable on this principle, but is likely to be problematic and complex to introduce and effect in practice.

The legitimate locus for public intervention in such matters is in the system of land tenure (obligations of stewardship in titles), the distribution of land (considerations of social justice and opportunity), and the statutory basis for land use planning and environmental protection (regulation of land use). Beyond that, people should be free to enjoy their property in whatever way they see fit.

Why, when people have many other things to do with their day, should they be expected to be part of an elaborate 'community consultation' exercise designed to legitimise local landed interests and satisfy the misguided political fashions of would-be land reforming politicians?

Room for Hope

The current agenda for land reform does, despite what I have just argued, contain much that is welcome. It is, however, deeply flawed in placing at its heart the fashionable view that the answer to current problems is to be found in appeals to the 'community of place'. This is a neat but unsophisticated way of avoiding confrontation with the power structures inherent in the division of land and in the institution of landownership. It is classic Gramscian hegemony – the 'elegant power' of the State dressed up as citizens' participation and empowerment.[9]

Perhaps there is hope, however. Lord Sewel, the Minister who chaired the committee which produced the report which forms the basis of the Scottish

Executive's policy, said in his foreword to it, 'These present recommendations are by no means the final word on land reform; they are a platform upon which we can build for the future.'[10]

Good! Because sooner or later we are going to need to get to grips with the real agenda for land reform. What does this agenda look like?

REFERENCES

1. *Partnership for Scotland – An Agreement for the First Scottish Parliament*, May 1999.
2. Scottish Office, 1999.
3. Scottish Executive, 1999.
4. Boyd, 1999a. See also 'Institutionalisation of Participation' in: Stiefel & Wolfe, 1994. 'The term institutionalisation implies, at a minimum, an intention on the part of the state to set rules for the game of participation. The state then encourages or protects certain kinds of participation by certain groups and discourages or prohibits other kinds of participation by other groups.'
5. Callander, 1987, p. 11.
6. Scottish Office, 1998b, p. 23.
7. Lord Sewel speaking on a visit to Knoydart on 27 August 1999. *The Herald* 28 August 1999.
8. Scottish Office, 1999, p. 4. This is the second of the two key visions for the future.
9. Elegant power is a term used by Gronemeyer (1992) to describe power which is 'unrecognisable, concealed, supremely inconspicuous' This, and the wider critique of development presented by Sachs (1992) has strong hints of Gramscian hegemony wherein the 'intellectual, moral and philosophical leadership provided by the class or alliance of classes and class fractions which is ruling, successfully achieves its objective of providing the fundamental outlook for the whole society.' (Bocock, 1986. p. 63).
10. Scottish Office, 1999, p. 1.

Chapter 6
A Land Reform Programme

*The central issue of people's participation is the
distribution of power – exercised by some people over
other people and by some classes over other classes –
any serious advocacy of increased participation implies
a redistribution of power in favour of those hitherto
powerless.*

MATTHIAS STIEFEL & MARSHALL WOLFE[1]

Having won the long struggle for a measure of home
rule, civil society now has the opportunity to develop a
programme of land reform which the new Parliament
can deliver. From arguing the case for land reform, we
are now in the more unfamiliar territory of what it
should actually involve. And it is here that there is much
more thinking to be done. What has already been
proposed by the Scottish Executive as a package of land
reform measures contains much that is worthwhile but
at its core is a flawed analysis of the problem and a
highly partial prescription of what to do about it.

Land reform in Scotland is about modernising the
current system of land tenure, challenging the division
of land, overthrowing the powerful elites who dominate
rural landownership, redistributing power over land,
and reforming the legal and financial instruments which
have been deployed to sustain and protect vested
interests. It is about improving accountability, about
adjusting the balance between public and private
interests, about creating economic opportunities for
people, and about sound stewardship of the
environment.

Land reform is not simply about tactical interventions in
the status quo. It involves reform in the way power is
derived, distributed, transferred and exercised.
It involves meaningful reform of the tenure system, the

ownership of land, the market in land, the division of land, the use of land, the fiscal status of land and the occupation of land. And it involves eliminating those characteristics of the current system which serve to perpetuate the status quo, which frustrate the public interest and which are antithetical to a just, fair and open society in a new Scotland. It is thus a highly political venture because in order to promote social, economic and environmental advancement, it needs to challenge and reorganise existing power structures.

Land reform is not simply about tactical interventions in the status quo. It involves reform in the way power is derived, distributed, transferred and exercised.

The aim of such a redistribution of power is to ensure that property rights are derived, distributed and exercised in ways which reflect the principles of fairness and the public interest at all stages. As a matter of political philosophy, it is far better to ensure that, as far as possible, the underlying framework of land tenure and ownership is conducive to the 'sustainable development of communities', so that by the time land use decisions are made, they do not become a power struggle between the community (relatively powerless) and the landowner (relatively powerful). And it is this basic concern with greater civic participation in land matters that suggests – without any anxious rationalisation over 'removing the land-based barriers to the sustainable development of communities'[2] – that a few simple but clear measures are justifiable to bring some semblance of social justice to bear on the land issue.

It should be stressed at this point that it is possible to support unreservedly the right of private citizens to enjoy private rights to land whilst at the same time promoting a wider allocation of those rights throughout society. Land reform which distributes power over the ownership and use of land more widely throughout the community is going to mean that we cease to need to get so worked up and anxious about the behaviour of individual landowners. Their influence will be significantly reduced beyond their own holdings. Increasingly, they will be part of a much broader and diverse grouping in society, rather than as in the case with large landowners, a tiny elite. This is healthy for landowners and healthy for democracy.

It is also worth mentioning that the argument for the redistribution of power encompasses the public sector, in particular that vast monolithic state body, the Forestry Commission, a body which James Hunter once described as 'being to Scottish forestry what collectivisation was to Soviet agriculture'.[3]

A programme of land reform should involve a range of measures that will extend democracy, opportunity and individual freedoms and rights within a clear framework of law and regulation. Such a programme needs to be developed strategically over a period of time. Land reform is both broad in terms of the range of changes it implies, and ongoing in terms of the need for a steady but sustained programme of change.

A Ten Point Agenda which embodies the kind of radical, reforming spirit with which the Scottish Parliament should be approaching land reform, would involve reform in the following areas:

- a new land tenure system
- system of land value tax
- national information system on land ownership and occupation
- limits to holding size
- agricultural tenant's right to buy allied with more flexible leasing arrangements

- residency obligations for landowners
- succession law reform
- a ban on offshore trusts and companies and private trusts
- reform of the land market
- action on the urban agenda.

1. Tenure

The abolition of feudal tenure represents a long overdue start to the modernisation of Scotland's land laws. As argued earlier though, there remains a big question mark over the philosophy and politics of replacing a conditional tenure system with an outright or absolute one. Moreover, the tenure system is about much more than abolition of feudalism. Robin Callander, in his book *How Scotland is Owned* subjects Scotland's land tenure system to a thorough-going and extensive review, analysis and critique which has subsequently been picked up on by Angus Calder and Alasdair Gray, two of Scotland's leading intellectuals.[4] He argues that we should go beyond simple abolition of the feudal system to create a new hierarchy of interests in Scotland's land tenure system, based upon the sovereignty of the people, the democracy of the Parliament and the property rights of land owners.

The ultimate goal for such a review is to develop a system of land tenure that retains the conditionality that the Crown currently represents as the locus of the public interest and that acknowledges that there are responsibilities as well as rights associated with the ownership of land. A conceptual model for such a new tenure system might look something like Figure 2 wherein rights derive from higher authorities and, reciprocally, responsibilities are acknowledged by each level to the one above.

It is this kind of conceptual thinking which needs to be

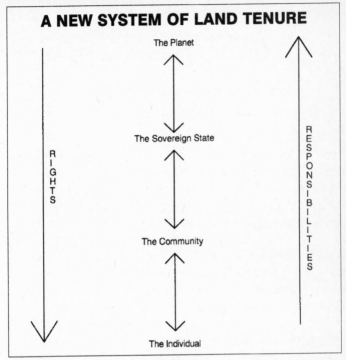

Figure 2

developed to inform those charged with reform of the feudal system (a process which has been devoid of any real debate) what it is that society wants out of a new tenure system, beyond the eradication of feudal superiors.

2. Land Values

It is a central argument of many economists and thinkers over the years that land plays a special role in the economy and that land taxes, together with energy and environmental taxes, are vital to reform of the economy as a whole.[5]

Since bare land is created by no one and is restricted in supply, its ownership confers economic power, in so far as all economic activity relies on land and land can be withheld from use. Land value taxation (LVT) or community ground rent is a form of public revenue levied on land values which are determined on the basis of bare land value (excluding all improvements) at current permitted uses. A high value parcel of land in the city centre would attract a high valuation by virtue of its valuable permitted use. This value is entirely due to its fortuitous location and the efforts of wider society in developing the surrounding area.

Land value taxation is not so much a tax as a fee paid by landowners in recognition of the exclusive rights which accompany land ownership and the community-created values embedded in parcels of land. The concept is designed to ease the burden of taxation on those things that create wealth, such as labour and capital, and increase it on land whose supply is fixed and held by private monopoly. Land value taxation can contribute substantially to public revenues and has been introduced in countries such as Denmark and New Zealand. In Britain it has been calculated that such measures could contribute as much as 44 per cent of all central and local government revenue and exceed that raised by income tax.[6] Its introduction would, therefore, allow the total elimination of taxes on income.

But whilst the introduction of LVT would do much to bring about a more responsive and socially just land market in urban areas, it remains unclear what its impact would be on rural landholdings. With relatively low land values over much of the countryside, the tax will be relatively modest and well within the ability of some of the richest people in Britain (and the world) to pay. In addition, many landowners of sporting estates are not rational decision makers in the economic sense. They pay massive capital sums for land of low rental value, and so will simply absorb any tax burden in their costs with minimal impact on the pattern of landownership.

3. Information

For too long the debate on land reform has been hampered by the lack of that most basic of commodities – hard, accurate information. In its absence the public, academics, policy makers, politicians and the media have been denied the most vital ingredients of research, analysis and debate. It is still difficult to assess the scale, location and character of landownership patterns in Scotland, never mind how they are evolving and changing over the years.

Commercial interests and public bodies have wasted vast amounts of time and money attempting to find out information on landownership and occupancy in the course of their everyday work. Utilities need to negotiate wayleaves. Local authorities need to survey new road alignments. Scientists need permission for wildlife survey work. Local people wish to contact landowners for a range of purposes. Emergency services need to contact landowners. Researchers need basic information to study the ownership and occupation of land. Many other people and groups, from film companies and outdoor activities organisers to mineral prospectors and developers have similar needs.

A new national land information system providing authoritative (though not definitive), accessible and comprehensive information on the ownership and occupancy of land is the answer. The Land Register will provide much of this information but it will not be complete until well into next century and possibly even beyond.[7]

But even with improved information, finding out that Footloose and Fancy Free Investments or Carskey

Aktiengesellschaft are the owners of the land you are interested in is not a great deal of assistance if you then find that they are registered at a PO Box in Panama or Liechtenstein! Until such legal entities are barred from holding title to land (see 8. in this chapter), we also need a statutory duty of disclosure of beneficial owners. Current proposals for a power to investigate such interests will be rendered toothless by the company law of Grand Cayman, Liberia and the British Virgin Islands.[8]

4. Holding Size

There appears to be a broad consensus that the extremely concentrated pattern of private landownership in Scotland is not in the public interest. As a matter of principle, it is unhealthy to have power over how land is used in so few hands. In economic terms it inhibits investment and enterprise. Socially and culturally it is disempowering. And environmentally, bad stewardship can have negative impacts over vast areas of land.

Current government proposals highlight two elements of a vision for the future.[9] The first is an 'increased diversity in the way land is owned and used which will lead to less concentration of ownership and management in a limited number of hands.' In the absence of any effective measures designed to achieve them, these are pious words.

In 1872 around 100 landowners owned half the privately owned land in Scotland. In 1970 this figure had risen to 313 and by 1999, to 343. At this rate there will, by the end of the 21st century, be 494 owners owning 50 per cent of the privately owned rural land in Scotland – hardly a revolution! Moreover as farm size gets bigger and new wealth increasingly funds the aggregation of other landholdings in Scotland, there is evidence that even this virtually imperceptible trend of the 20th century towards a less concentrated pattern of ownership may now be beginning to slow down and indeed reverse.

It doesn't take an arithmetical genius to work out that a desire to see even a modest reduction in landowning monopolies will fail hopelessly unless clear policies are adopted to reduce the scale of landholdings. So far nothing has been proposed which will achieve this. In order to tackle the problem it is necessary first of all to tackle the root causes of the situation, for example succession law and taxation policies. However the landowning monopoly has been crafted and defended so carefully that further radical measures will be necessary to generate the initial momentum.

It doesn't take an arithmetical genius to work out that a desire to see even a modest reduction in landowning monopolies will fail hopelessly unless clear policies are adopted to reduce the scale of landholdings.

Landowning interests vehemently oppose any measures designed to dismantle large holdings although such a stance is rather undermined by the almost universal practice of landowners themselves who, despite their political opposition to the break up of holdings, seem happy to maximise their gains when it comes to selling large properties by offering the land in separate lots. It is one of the few occasions when private interests under the current system come anywhere near matching public interests.

Given that it is common practice to lot property, it should not be too contentious to insist on a compulsory lotting of large properties when they come up for sale. Such a measure should be tied to legal prohibition on any individual accumulation of property over a certain scale. There is also an argument for insisting on compliance with such restrictions by a set date (say in 25 years or one generation) regardless of whether the property has been sold. Again there is sufficient evidence that, since such a practice appears commonplace already on landed estates where, typically, large numbers of family trusts own separate blocks of land, it should not prove to be an exceptional burden even for the largest estates, even if it does involve simply parcelling the estate among members of the same family.

This kind of proposal tends to prompt indignant protests about cost and bureaucracy from landed interests. But increasing the number of landowners means a greater diversity and scale of meaningful investment in the countryside and greater stability in the institution of landownership. In short, it is actually quite good news both for departing landowners and incoming ones.

5. Tenant Right-to-Buy

A striking feature of agricultural holdings in Scotland is the high proportion (30 per cent) of farms which are tenanted under agricultural leases. The rest of Western Europe abolished tenant farming centuries ago. Experience in countries such as Denmark shows how real land reform can provide more people with a stake in the land, ensure the availability of land at modest prices to newcomers and ensure that Danish agriculture remains amongst the most competitive in the world. Denmark turned its back on the landowner-tenant model in the late 18th century and has seen no reason to return to it.

Giving tenant farmers a statutory right to buy the farm upon which generations of their family may have lived and worked is a modest but vital measure. No farmer would be obliged to buy their holding but those who felt that such a move might offer them a better future would be entitled to exercise the same right as, for example, crofters and council house tenants now enjoy.

Tenant right-to-buy was the measure which ended
landlordism in Ireland, where its loss has not been
obviously associated with a plunge into rural poverty
and economic collapse – quite the reverse in fact. And it
is interesting that the idea is even supported by a
landowner in Scotland whose family has held their land
for as long as 800 years. Lord Robert-Mercer-Nairne,
owner of Meiklour Estate in Perthshire wrote recently:

'There is a feeling in Scotland that too few own too
much; that we are stuck with an historical pattern of
landownership that is no longer appropriate. Giving
secure tenants the right to buy their farms is likely to be
the only way out of this log-jam.'[10]

It would be hard to put the argument more eloquently.
Such a move should be allied to new arrangements to
make existing tenancies more flexible by allowing a
greater diversity of economic activity by tenants (e.g.
forestry and tourism), the strengthening of existing
tenant's rights and the introduction of new and more
flexible leasing arrangements for land for new entrants
to agriculture. Such entrants would not, it should be
stressed enjoy the same right to buy as existing tenants.
The right-to-buy would be restricted to those tenants
who, under the existing Agricultural Holdings Act, held
a tenancy at a defined retrospective date.

Such a qualification nails dead the claim, promoted
vigorously by the SLF (and indeed repeated by the
Scottish Office themselves[11]) that landowners would
cease entirely to let more land and that the supply of
land for rent would dry up. No tenant entering any new
tenancy after the right-to-buy legislation was introduced
would qualify for the right-to-buy under that legislation.

A right-to-buy for farming tenants would be offered to a
defined range of people in terms of the nature of their
tenancy and the length of time over which it had been
held. Such an opportunity would be retroactive and

would apply only to those who meet the criteria at an appointed date (probably the date of the introduction of the legislation). No one taking out a new tenancy would be covered by the legislation. It would not apply to them and so there is no reason (other than a suspicion that at some future date they might also be given the right-to-buy) for landowners to be reluctant to let land. Suspicions over future intentions can be overcome by introducing a new form of tenancy which is fixed term and which explicitly denies the right to take possession of the land in future.

6. Residency

Absentee landlords have attracted much enmity in debates about land reform. Indeed the term has become an essential part of the land reform lexicon. Unfortunately, despite railing against absentee lairds, the politicians and the media (who seem to love the term) have seldom argued that something should actually be done about it.

First let us get the argument straight. Absentee landownership is corrosive culturally and socially. It generates and sustains the 'estate factor' and that debilitating culture of mean-spirited and supine yes men who, in indulging their own over-blown egos in doing the lairds' bidding, have probably done more harm to communities than the landlords themselves.
Far preferable a community in which there are many owners of land living on the land they have responsibility for managing.

Permanent residency on the land one owns should and must be a legal obligation. It already is for crofting tenants and agricultural tenants: the tenant is subjected to a battery of regulation and obligation whilst the ownership regime is curiously free of such inconveniences.

The SLF and their spin doctors claim that absentee

landowners need to be away somewhere else in order to earn income which is then invested in their properties. It is an endearing notion. One has visions of poverty-stricken landowners having to beat the long and weary road to Edinburgh, London, Guernsey, and Grand Cayman to earn a crust when in fact the reality is precisely the opposite. Most absentee owners originate from outwith the area in which they own land and visit it on an occasional basis for holidays or a bit of hunting, fishing and shooting.

The landholders who are on the long and weary road to Glasgow and beyond in search of income are much more likely to be crofters. And yet, perversely, the Government is currently taking action under the powers of the Crofting Acts which could lead to their eventual removal as crofting tenants.[12]

If it is deemed good enough for crofters, why should the legislation not be applied to landowners who control hundreds and thousands of acres? Scotland needs rid of absentee landlords.

7. Succession Law Reform

As argued in Chapter 2, the preservation of our vast feudal estates has been made possible almost exclusively by the arrangements surrounding the inheritance of landed property. Unlike other forms of property (stocks and shares, furniture and vehicles) which are classified as moveables, land is defined as immoveable or heritable property; the legal rights children and spouses have over a deceased person's estate, which can be invoked in cases of testate succession, only apply to moveable property. We are one of the few countries which recognises such a division. Nothing can be done to challenge the wishes of the deceased when it comes to land. Given a long history of primogeniture and a slow turnover of land, it is not surprising that this still tends to favour the eldest male child.

*Calm down – absentee landowners have nothing to fear
– it's those damn absentee crofters we're after!*

Right across Europe, the abolition of feudalism and the rights granted to family members to inherit land have been responsible for a pluralistic, small scale pattern of landownership and the elimination of the larger landed estates. It could do the same in Scotland since the Scottish Law Commission have already published proposals for the elimination of any distinction between heritable and moveable property.[13] This reform could therefore be acted upon relatively quickly.

This measure would signal more powerfully than any other the intent to do something radical about the distribution of landowning power. Such a reform could adopt a range of options for the division of heritable property, ranging from equal and mandatory division, to optional equal division, to succession by the eldest child allied with compensation for other children. It is the principle which matters, however, since nothing symbolises more strongly the institutionalisation of landed power in few hands than the arrangements for its inheritance.

8. Offshore Trusts & Companies and Private Trusts

The ownership of land in Scotland must in future be allied to accountability, openness, fairness and opportunities for all. One of the most inimical characteristics of the system is the ability of those who enjoy landed power to secrete their assets and identity behind a cloak of anonymity in legal personalities designed to avoid tax and secure the line of inheritance beyond their lifetime. None of these actions is in the public interest.

Offshore trusts, blind trusts and private trusts are the favoured ways of keeping landed assets secure and free of tax, of denying the public the right to know who really owns the land, and of ensuring that landed families can protect their assets in the face of incompetency and bankruptcy. Private trusts sterilise the land for future generations whose aspirations and needs may be very different to those of today. They perpetuate landed privilege and a concentrated pattern of ownership at a time when opportunities to access land should be expanded.

Around one third of Scotland is now owned through such devices. Offshore trusts are used not only by anonymous individuals but also by some of Scotland's leading landed families who, not content with their substantial landed assets, seek every way they can to avoid paying any tax. None of us is obliged to organise our affairs in such a way that exposes us to paying too much tax and neither should we be. But that does not mean that we should condone the kind of devices that enable the wealthiest individuals to avoid tax while the poorest in society have little choice but to pay their fair share.

One of the most inimical characteristics of the system is the ability of those who enjoy landed power to secrete their assets and identity behind a cloak of anonymity in legal personalities designed to avoid tax and secure the line of inheritance beyond their lifetime.

Moreover, in recent years an increasing number of landowners have been receiving thousands, sometimes millions of pounds in public money through agricultural and forestry grants and conservation agreements. These payments have been made to companies and trusts in Panama, Liechtenstein and the Bahamas. We are not entitled to know who is benefiting from this largesse, nor can we expect a return on our investment through capital taxation. A situation where taxpayer's money can be paid out to any anonymous individual or company anywhere in the world is scandalous and corrupt and flies in the face of the prudent and accountable use of taxpayers' money.

Anyone owning land should be entitled to register title only in forms which serve the public interest, namely individuals and, in certain circumstances, companies governed by the Companies Act. All offshore trusts and private trusts should be deemed incompetent legal personalities to own land. The land market should be restricted to bona fide individuals who are prepared to be open about their identity, pay their fair share of tax, and allow future generations the freedom to determine in their interests how land is held and used.

9. The Land Market

An unregulated market in land has allowed land to be treated as any other form of commodity: those who control the monopoly in land can dictate the timing and extent of its release, anyone from anywhere can buy as much as is on offer, and there is virtually no accountability or opportunity for the wider community to intervene or register an interest. Land is traded, often in secret, to people whose motives may be speculative, who need not demonstrate any ability or competence to manage it, and who may not have the slightest interest in local affairs, local development, or local culture.

As Jan van der Ploeg from the Agricultural University of Wageningen in the Netherlands observed, 'This is wild-west capitalism. One of the most valuable assets for the future, the land, can be bought and sold at will. Elsewhere in Europe this is not the case.'[14]

This lack of regulation has led to the situation where communities are completely powerless to influence the nature, character or motivation of those who own land in and around settlements. This lack of regulation is of less importance in the kind of situation which exists in much of western Europe where there's a healthy balance of public ownership, social and co-operative ownership, communal ownership and small-scale private ownership. It is of major concern where a handful of owners control the use of land over large areas. As a catalogue of cases has shown, an unregulated market and a concentrated pattern of ownership leads sooner or later to problems.

At this stage it is worth stressing that the debate is about the extent of regulation and the kinds of functions this should fulfil. The principle is already established in crofting that assignations of tenancy, de-crofting, amalgamations and even the competence of an occupier are subject to regulation. The anomaly that exists is that such regulation is deemed to be appropriate for a few acres of bog and rock above Newtonmore when at the same time the transfer of 40,000 acres of internationally important land in Glen Feshie can be traded in the VIP lounge of Heathrow airport with no scrutiny whatsoever!

The detail of such regulation awaits further debate. Limits to holding size and residency obligations have already been cited. The Scottish Executive's proposals provide communities with the right-to-buy under certain circumstances. But the real challenge is to open the land market to all sorts of diverse arrangements, from individuals wanting a few acres, to new farmers wanting to secure a modest holding, to groups within communities wishing to initiate business ventures or develop forestry projects, to housing associations wanting some land for housing, and, yes, to whole communities wanting to control land assets.

Critical to such arrangements will be the development of mechanisms such as a public right of pre-emption and enhanced compulsory purchase powers. Compulsory purchase powers need to be made available for a much wider range of purposes than at present and need to be easier to use. The burden of proof should be on the existing owner to demonstrate a greater social need for the land, particularly where only a small part of a much larger holding is involved. The handling of such cases should utilise methods such as Citizens' Juries to make recommendations, and use arbitration to resolve disputes. Finally, land purchased compulsorily should attract levels of compensation which are just and fair to both parties, taking into account the existing use of the land as well as the intended use of the land.

Regulating the market in land, which is by definition a monopoly market, is vital to achieving the goals of land reform. Far from being bureaucratic and cumbersome, as Government has argued,[15] such regulation would be relatively straightforward and simple to implement; it would bring new opportunities to many more people than the current monopoly of vested interest dressed up as the free market in land.

10. The Urban Agenda

Land reform is generally portrayed as a rural issue. Given the peculiar nature and distribution of land in rural Scotland, the media focus on places like Assynt, Eigg and Knoydart, and the classical definition of land reform, this is perhaps not surprising. But land reform is not just about rural land, for the following reasons:

- All land in Scotland, rural and urban (and marine) is the legitimate concern of all the people of Scotland.

- The planning system – the main publicly accountable system for determining land use – affects urban land far more than rural land, but continues to fail urban communities wishing to have more control over their environment.

- Urban land use affects greater numbers of people; reform of the planning system, introduction of land value taxation, access to the countryside, and measures to allow repopulation of rural areas will all benefit urban dwellers.

- Feudal tenure and the law of the tenement affect urban interests far more than rural interests.

- Community and co-operative ownership or management of public sector housing, and indeed of public sector green spaces such as parks and recreation facilities, is the urban equivalent of community ownership and management in rural areas.

There will always be an urban Scotland and a rural Scotland. The tragedy is that they have become dislocated culturally, politically and economically from one another through the forces of industrialisation, landownership patterns, restrictive planning and the burden of taxation. Land reform provides the opportunity to negotiate and settle a new relationship both between Scottish society and those who own land, and between urban and rural Scotland. Such a settlement must be based on social and economic justice, opportunity, mutual respect and trust, and wider access to and control of how land in urban and rural areas is owned, used and managed.

A Wider Land Reform Agenda

There are of course many other areas of land reform which need addressed. These include crofting tenure, public access, marine resource management, game and fisheries resource management, and reform of the arrangements and institutions associated with the ownership of public land.

Beyond this there is a further range of broader land policy issues. These include the question of affordable housing, communal hutting schemes like the one at Carbeth, participatory planning processes, social and co-operative financing and support arrangements for

land ventures, greater local control and management of
natural resources, control of mineral exploitation, and
recreational land use (including hunting) and the future
of sporting estates.

These are a vital part of a wider policy towards land.
They should not, however, be confused with the core
business of land reform, which is to reform existing
power structures. Only once this has been done can the
wider gains from a more equitable, open and
accountable system of land tenure be realised.

So Will This Happen?

Very little of the above agenda is currently under
consideration by the main political parties. Indeed,
much of it has been explicitly rejected in a rather tetchy
and petulant fashion. The Scottish Parliament does
provide opportunities for deepening and widening the
debate. But we need more than the mechanics of a new
democracy. We also need greater civic engagement in the
issue and here the recently established Scottish Land
Reform Convention will have a vital role to play in
leading the debate within civil society.

Before coming to a final conclusion, it might be helpful
to present the arguments most frequently deployed
against land reform and provide some answers to them.
In many cases they will be seen to be myths and
propaganda designed to promote thinly-veiled self-
interest.

REFERENCES

1. Stiefel & Wolfe, 1994. p. 4.
2. Scottish Office, 1999. This is the objective for land reform according to the Land Reform Policy Group's paper 'Recommendations for Action'.
3. Hunter, 1992
4. Calder & Gray, 1999.
5. Robertson, 1998, summarises the wider case for new economics and Harrison, 1998, the specific case for the collection of the rental value of land.
6. Banks, 1989.
7. The Land Register was established in 1979 to replace the older Register of Sasines which has been in existence since 1617. It is being introduced on a county by

county basis and will cover all of Scotland by 2003. Transfer to the Land Register, however, is only triggered by a sale for value. Much land therefore will not transfer from Sasines to the Land Register for many decades (and some may take a century or more). Scope exists to increase the triggers for transfer (e.g. upon inheritance) and to make registration compulsory perhaps at some point in future when only a small number of properties remain unregistered.

8. Scottish Office (1999) proposes that there should be 'a reserve power to enable the Secretary of State to investigate beneficial ownership of land where a clear need for such information exists in the public interest.' This is an attempt to address long-standing demands to eliminate secrecy surrounding who owns land. It is a doomed attempt, however. Some of this information is already available in the public domain (though it can be difficult to get hold of) and therefore there is no need for any powers of investigation. But the information that is difficult to obtain is the beneficial ownership of offshore companies and trusts and no reserve power of government will penetrate the disclosure laws of Grand Cayman and Liberia! The only option is to legally require any owner of land to disclose their beneficial ownership.

9. Scottish Office, 1999, p. 4.
10. Lord Robert Mercer-Nairne, *The Scotsman* 26 June 1998.
11. Scottish Office, 1998b, p. 65.
12. Crofters Commission Annual Report 1998/99. See also reports in *The Scotsman* and *The Herald*, 16 June 1999.
13. Scottish Law Commission, 1990.
14. Jan van der Ploeg speaking on Eorpa, BBC Scotland, 19 October 1995.
15. See Scottish Office, 1998b. p. 18. Also see Chapter 9 of this publication for a response to the charge.

Chapter 7
Ah But!

'Small-scale landholdings are inefficient'

No they are not – precisely the opposite, in fact. Efficiency does not depend on the scale of ownership: it is the scale of management that matters. Western Europe provides the model. There, a more pluralistic pattern of ownership has created a large body of self motivated people, willing to invest and diversify. Consider for example the forest industry. In Scotland we have a state forest sector – monolithic, inflexible and distant – and a private sector which is increasingly composed of various speculative investment scams and offshore company tax breaks none of which contributes anything to locally-based rural development.

In much of the rest of Europe small farmers are organised into powerful co-operative federations capable of competing in global markets. In Norway, for example, there are 55,000 members of the Norwegian Forest Owners' Federation. They control 75 per cent of the timber market in Norway and together they built up Norske Skog, Norway's biggest forest products company in which the Federation still has a 36 per cent stake. Across the border in Sweden is Södra, Europe's largest producer of chlorine-free wood pulp, which is owned and run by 27,000 forest farmers.

Across the border in Sweden is Södra, Europe's largest producer of chlorine-free wood pulp, which is owned and run by 27,000 forest farmers.

Despite the best efforts of parts of the agricultural industry, Scotland has failed to emulate anything like the phenomenal social economy of co-operative marketing, processing, retailing and banking which is commonplace all over Europe.

Smaller landholdings promote greater levels of investment than larger ones. They promote greater diversity in approach to business. They promote stability, individual liberty, and co-operative strength and flexibility. There is nothing inefficient about small landholdings.

'Large landowners are benevolent and put lots of money into the local economy'

This is an argument frequently deployed in defence of Highland landownership in particular. Much landholding in the region consists of sporting estates. As forms of conspicuous consumption they were never designed to be profitable concerns and continue to pay scant regard to the need to invest in tangible economic activity, as opposed to the financing of recreational hunting and of leisured enjoyment.

As the independent Chairmen of Scotland's Rating Valuation Tribunals concluded in a damning indictment of the Tory Government's abolition of sporting rates, 'These sporting estates change hands for capital sums which far exceed their letting value and which are of no benefit to the area, and are often bought because there are tax advantages to the purchaser, not necessarily in the UK. The local staff are poorly paid, their wages bearing no relation to the capital invested in the purchase price, and it is not unusual to find a man responsible for an investment in millions being paid a basic agricultural wage. Many of the estates use short-term labour during the sporting season, leaving the taxpayer to pay their staff from the dole for the rest of the year. Estates can in many cases be deliberately run at a loss, thereby reducing their owner's tax liability to central funds elsewhere in the UK'.

But even this is not the whole story. Sporting estates do not lose money overall – quite the opposite. Since 1980 they have appreciated in value by over 8 per cent

annually, more than sufficient to indulge in the revenue
costs of recreational capitalism. Many owners pay no
tax on these capital gains as they are registered offshore,
the environmental cost of an excessive population of red
deer is substantial, and there is the opportunity cost of
other activities and investment opportunities denied by
monopolistic landholdings.

**'Demand for land reform is driven by a few cases
of bad landowners'**

To an extent this is true, but the implication that land
reform can be reduced simply to such a issue is
ludicrous. Politicians play on such notions ('Good
landowners have nothing to fear from land reform,'
they declare – and good dictators have nothing to fear
from democracy?!) Land reform is not about punishing
bad landowners (in the private or public sector). There
will always be bad landowners just as there are bad bus
drivers, journalists, builders, and plumbers. The real
issue is to reduce the impact of their activities by
eliminating their ability to exercise power over such vast
areas of land by denying the opportunity to hold large
estates. A few bad landowners matter much less if their
impact is restricted to a few modest holdings, as
opposed to half a county!

Framing the debate in these terms (either by politicians
or landowners) does raise the awkward question of
what, if anything, to do about so-called bad
landowners. The last thing the new Scotland needs is an
army of bureaucrats assessing landowners on the quality
of their land management. So where power is being
exercised in anti-social ways the answer is not to
attempt to confront or challenge that power by the use
of a big stick, but to eliminate its existence in the first
place. Taking a topical example, there would never have
been the problem there was on the Island of Eigg if all
the residents owned their own homes and if the island
as a whole was divided into 10–20 individual farms.

'It's not who owns land that matters but how it is managed'

This has become the mantra of those who do not wish either to acknowledge or to address the question of land tenure and landownership. It has been regularly deployed by all political parties, by senior civil servants, by Quango bosses, and with monotonous regularity by landowners and, in particular, by their lickspittle colleagues, the land agents, factors and lawyers.

No one denies that it matters how land is managed and used, but to suggest that how land is owned (the tenure system), how it is divided (the pattern of landownership), and who owns it (the range of bodies and individuals who own land) is irrelevant, is absurd. All these factors are connected: how land is managed is influenced by how it is used, who is using it, why they are using it and what power they have to use it.

This analysis of the land question is a device designed to protect vested interests and to deflect unpalatable and uncomfortable debate about land reform. If who owns land really is so unimportant, and it is management that really matters, can we all have a share please?

'It is not surprising so few people own land – much of it is of poor quality'

This argument is often based on the value of land in agricultural terms. Marginal land, it is alleged, needs to be held in large parcels to be economically viable. But a brief look at the structure of agricultural holdings in Scotland reveals that, far from the poorest land being in the largest holdings, the opposite is the case: the smallest holdings are crofts on the west coast and the largest are the big farms of Berwickshire. This pattern is repeated in Ireland also – why? Because historically, capitalist farmers on good land have expanded by borrowing whereas poorer peasant farmers have been pushed to the congested margins.

The scale of holdings has as much to do with wider social, political and economic factors than simply land quality. Of these, probably the most single significant factor is almost 900 years of primogeniture which has perpetuated vast estates, often in defiance of rational economic logic which would suggest their division and allocation to the wider community.

Arguments about land quality confuse and frustrate debate and action to dismantle landed power. They are also pretty misleading when, for example, on the poorest land imaginable (on hilltops and moorland) one can earn an annual rental of £3,000 for a mobile phone mast (that's equivalent to a rental of £20,000 per acre!). Poor land today is good land tomorrow!

'Landowners are good to the local community – they provide sites for swimming pools and for health centres and donate money to local charities'
Scotland's landowning classes sometimes do 'donate' land. This follows a long historical tradition of patrician benevolence. If you own 10,000 acres or 100,000 acres (which in many cases you didn't pay for), are we expected to fall over ourselves in gratitude for donating a quarter or a half acre? Social justice alone would suggest that large landowners with tens of thousands (or even thousands) of acres have a moral obligation to release land to the community for their needs.

And what of this wider charity which the nouveau riche are particularly keen on in order to ingratiate themselves to local people, politicians and the media to lend some legitimacy to their sprawling acres? It is welcome, of course, but what dignity and self-respect is afforded society when such acts become indispensable in the absence of public investment? And what have such acts of charity got to do with the rights and wrongs of the current division of land? Wealthy landowners donating money to local causes is no more of a justification for the current land monopoly than are earnest attempts to learn Gaelic, the provision of a field for the local agricultural show, or being nice to people in the street.

'Regulation of the land market is bureaucratic'

Any form of regulation involves a bureaucracy. The question is whether the regulation brings net benefits or frustrates and retards development and innovation. The most dynamic and stable land-based economies tend to be those where there are many occupants, pursuing a diversity of activities, creating a diverse economy, making maximum use of indigenous knowledge, investing in land capability and businesses and with a stake in the land. If, as I argue, regulation can promote that, then it is to be welcomed, particularly as it relies, not on an army of bureaucrats interfering with individuals' freedoms but on a simple and clear framework of law. Many of the measures proposed here do not involve any bureaucracy at all – the reform of succession law, for example. Others can be secured through conditions attached to the process of conveyancing and registration of title.

Wealthy landowners donating money to local causes is no more of a justification for the current land monopoly than are earnest attempts to learn Gaelic, the provision of a field for the local agricultural show, or being nice to people in the street.

Even regulating the market in land, potentially the most demanding aspect of land reform, is a modest undertaking. From 1990 to 1998 there have been, on average, around 200 farms, 20 estates and 30 forest properties advertised on the open market. Allowing for sales off the open market one might double these figures. With around 500 sales of land above a threshold of around 100 acres taking place a year (no one is suggesting the need to regulate small-scale sales such as houses and gardens), the effort required to regulate would be not be formidable at all. The annual regulatory case load of the Crofters Commission, for example, is measured in the thousands, and any regulatory arrangements for landownership would be relatively modest by comparison.

'Interfering with private property rights is a breach of human rights and contrary to European law'

Private property rights have not only been extensively interfered with in the past but perfect authority exists to redefine them in the future.

Article 1 of the European Convention on Human Rights states:

'Every natural or legal person is entitled to the peaceful enjoyment of his possessions. No one shall be deprived of his possessions except in the public interest and subject to the conditions provided for by law and by the general principles of international law. The preceding provisions shall not, however, in any way impair the right of a State to enforce such laws as it deems necessary to control the use of property in accordance with the general interest or to secure the payment of taxes or other contributions or penalties.'

'Public interest' is the key phrase and has already been tested in the English Courts. In 1986 the trustees of the Second Duke of Westminster argued that the Leasehold Reform Act of 1967, which enabled tenants under long leases to purchase their freehold interest at what were regarded as favourable rates, breached this Article. Although the court recognised that the Act did indeed deprive the applicants of their possessions, it also recognised that 'the compulsory transfer of property from one individual to another may, in principle, be considered to be 'in the public interest', if the taking is effected in pursuance of legitimate social policies'.

No less a body than the Scottish Law Commission have cited this case to support their contention that the abolition of the feudal system in Scotland, 'long after it has been abolished in other European countries is, in our view, a legitimate policy'. Furthermore, 'We do not consider that the abolition of the superiority interest in itself should give rise to entitlement to compensation.'[2]

In practice the history of land reform is littered with examples of the redefinition of property rights from the Crofting Act of 1886 to the Town and Country Planing Act of 1947 and the Land Tenure Reform (Scotland) Act of 1974. Since the restriction of individual private property rights usually involves the expansion of everyone else's, land reform measures will justifiably continue to redefine property rights in the public interest.

REFERENCES

1. Dewing, 1994. Report prepared for the Rating Valuation Chairman's Committee. Cited in the *West Highland Free Press*.

2. Scottish Law Commission, 1991, pp. 136–137.

Chapter 8
Conclusions

We have long been in the habit in Scotland of bemoaning the more obvious excesses of our current landownership system. Newspaper libraries bulge with condemnatory articles about the way in which this or that community has had its prospects blighted as a result of finding its entire future dependent on the whims of the crook, the charlatan or the speculator who has become its laird. And as each new scandal comes along, there is never any lack of politicians, local or national, to denounce its perpetrators and to declare that such a thing must never be permitted to happen again.

But it has happened again. And it will happen again. And again. And again. It will go on happening, in fact, until Scots, nationally and collectively, set the ownership of land on a new legislative basis.

JAMES HUNTER[1]

New Opportunities?

There is now the opportunity to create a very different future for Scotland. In our towns and cities we need to reclaim and reassert the right to use land in the public interest. The collection of the rental value of land can end the worst excesses of speculation. Greater participation and local democracy can enhance public amenities. Innovative design, co-operative frameworks, and devolved responsibility and authority can begin to solve our shocking housing availability and condition.

In rural areas, prosperity and security can be promoted by providing many, many more individuals, groups and communities with a stake in the ownership and use of land. No one has ever suggested that land reform is the single solution to the future well-being of rural Scotland. It is, however, a process which can remove

barriers (to securing affordable housing for example)
and create a wide range of opportunities for investment,
employment and recreation and which can contribute to
the development of a stable, self-confident society.

To achieve this it will be necessary to conduct a far-
reaching and radical reform of the laws and other
arrangements governing the ownership and use of land.
And here is is worth recognising that for too long,
landowners have been viewed as targets for much that is
wrong in Scotland. But landowners are not the problem.
As Winston Churchill argued whilst campaigning for
land reform earlier this century (yes, he was a land
reformer too!):

'It is not the individual I attack, it is the system. It is not
the man who is bad, it is the law which is bad. It is not
the man who is blameworthy for doing what the law
allows and what other men do, it is the State which
would be blameworthy were it not to endeavour to
reform the law and correct the practice. We do not want
to punish the landlord. We want to alter the law.'[2]

Reforming the system may involve going beyond the
measures outlined in this book. The way in which land
is traded, used, abused, financed, subsidised and
developed has reached levels which no civilised society
should tolerate. The following advertisement recently
appeared in the *Financial Times*:

For the Price of a Flat in Fulham
you can create your own wooded estate
paid for by government grants

**Net income for 10–15 years with Inheritance Tax/
Capital Gains Tax advantages
Protect the environment and establish new
wildlife habitats
Sporting and family enjoyment**[3]

This scheme, the Farm Woodland Scheme, is intended to assist farmers to diversify into forestry – a commendable and worthwhile endeavour – but is being promoted as a get rich quick scheme for wealthy investors who can buy a farm, be paid to plant trees on it, enjoy a government financed net annual income of 7–12 per cent of capital invested, and a capital asset which again is tax-free![4]

There should not be much bother finding takers. As the troubled farmers leave the hills, the 'Caledonian Initiative' hits the road visiting Hong Kong, Singapore and Kuala Lumpur to drum up interest in Scottish land. The solicitors, Tods Murray and land agents John Clegg have created a travelling one-stop-shop where rich businessmen will be shown the range of land for sale in Scotland.[5]

Nowhere else in Europe could such an unregulated market hold sway over so much land. What is really scandalous is that so much public money can get thrown at Scottish farms, not for Scottish farmers, but for people already seriously rich who can create a nice little sporting estate and holiday retreat on the back of British taxpayers money and tax breaks.

Political Realities

Radical land reform advances two relatively simple ideas, namely public accountability and the redistribution of power. If this is to have any chance of taking place, land reform needs to enjoy the oxygen and participation heralded by the new politics in Scotland. It would be enormously depressing if the new Scottish Executive assumed that just because current government proposals have been the subject of limited and selective Scottish Office consultation that they are the most appropriate package of land reform for Scotland.

It should also be noted that the core recommendation, the community right-to-buy, has not even been subjected to genuine consultation. Donald Dewar, in his McEwen Lecture in Aviemore on 4 September 1998 stated quite categorically, 'I wish to be absolutely clear that I regard this right (the community right-to-buy) as an essential prerequisite of land reform. The problems must be overcome and the right must be established.'[6] So much for the integrity of the consultation document he then launched inviting views on such a measure! No wonder that there is widespread disillusionment with what has been described as a radical package of land reform measures.

James Hunter argued recently that 'the process on which we are embarking could, if we make it so, be far-reaching in its implications... It could certainly result in very basic alterations in the current pattern of ownership and control.'[7] Whether or not such alterations are well in hand by the end of the first or even the second or third terms of a Scottish Parliament is open to doubt. The much vaunted community right-to-buy will certainly not achieve such an outcome.

It is easy to be impressed by the heady rhetoric of politicians spouting forth on the land question and how they are going to solve it, particularly since land reform has been so bleak a prospect for so long.

It is easy to be impressed by the heady rhetoric of politicians spouting forth on the land question and how they are going to solve it, particularly since land reform has been so bleak a prospect for so long. And it is not to doubt the sincerity with which politicians from the progressive end of politics have embraced land reform, to question whether indeed land reform, as currently conceived, is going to have any impact beyond perhaps at most reigning in the worst cases of abuse, empowering crofters, and promoting a rather more co-operative disposition among the landed classes.

The role of the Scottish Parliament is to provide a framework of land law which satisfies basic human needs, protects and enhances the environment, is socially just, equitable and fair. It should provide opportunities for individuals and communities to develop economically, socially and culturally. That will not come about without a principled and determined willingness to confront the power structures embodied in the current system of land law and in one of the most concentrated pattern of private landownership anywhere in the world.

But who is going to do this? Contemporary politics is constrained by its loss of faith in political ideology and principle. Instead it operates by responding in a managerial kind of a way to pressure from civil society. The Land Reform Policy Group is a classic case. Civil society (and a few individual politicians) had been pressing for land reform for a long time. Government responded by setting up a group of predominantly civil servants to develop a programme of reform which could be presented as radical and effective but did not in fact change matters a great deal. It was an exclusive process of policy development which ignored history, ignored the overseas experience (not only in western Europe, but also in Latin America and Africa), marginalised dissent and suppressed criticism of its assumptions.

Land reform cannot be left to politicians operating in a normative and intellectually bereft environment. For over 150 years government has failed to support civil society's efforts to wrest control of land.[8] The mid-19th century efforts of the Chartists and the National Land Company to redistribute land failed. Later that century, demands by James Bryce MP for public access to land were rejected. For much of this century, civic groups, whether crofters, tenant's groups, community groups, conservationists or recreationalists, have had to fight to assert and promote their interests. The State has stood idly by.

Instead of advancing notions of democracy, social justice or environmental stewardship as the underpinning of land reform, Government has fallen for the fashionable concept of community. In the hands of politicians this has been articulated as a rather unsophisticated idea which conceals the simple fact that it it the unequal distribution of power which lies at the root of the problems arising from the division and use of land in Scotland.

Such monumental failure highlights the historic inability to see the land problem for what it is – an issue of power relations governed by Scotland's land laws. This poses a real challenge for the Scottish Parliament. It is likely that civil society, through the Scottish Land Reform Convention and other initiatives, will again have to keep the pressure on Parliament to deliver a policy agenda which redistributes political and economic power over land, creates more democratic control over how land is used, and develops a culture in Scotland which gives individual citizens and communities far greater opportunities to benefit from the land resource.

And opportunity is the key. A framework of land law which imposes inflexible and bureaucratic arrangements will not provide for the wide range of circumstances it is likely to have to deal with and is likely to meet with substantial opposition. A new framework which provides for greater accountability and participation in decisions about land will work if people have the choice as to whether to exercise such powers. In many cases they will not be necessary. But in many cases they will. Land reform is emphatically not simply a programme of removing 'land-based barriers to sustainable rural development'[9] but a major political reform which is capable of transforming Scotland just as similar reforms changed for ever the lives of those in Ireland, Norway, France, Denmark, the Netherlands, Mexico, Peru, Taiwan and China.

At long last we are in the fortunate position of being able to join the growing international land reform movement. It is time to rise to the challenge presented by land reform, and to embark upon a programme of political reform which allows civic Scotland to develop a new understanding of its relationship with the land of Scotland – an understanding based upon sovereignty, democracy, social justice and stewardship.

REFERENCES

1 Hunter, 1996. Foreword to Wightman, 1996b.

2. From a speech delivered by Winston Churchill at the King's Theatre, Edinburgh, 17 July 1909.

3. *Financial Times,* 6/7 March Weekend p. xiv.

4. Tilhill Economic Forestry Ltd., 1999.

5. *Scotland on Sunday,* 31 January 1999

6. Dewar, 1998. p. 19.

7. Hunter, 1998. p. 34

8. Boyd, 1999b.

9. Scottish Office, 1999. p. 4.

SOME FURTHER READING

A.S. Armstrong & A.S. Mather, 1983. *Land Ownership and Land Use in the Scottish Highlands*. O'Dell Memorial Monograph No. 13. Department of Geography, University of Aberdeen.

R. Banks, (ed.), 1989. *Costing the Earth*. Shepheard-Walwyn, London.

J. Bateman, 1883. *The Great Landowners of Great Britain and Ireland*. Harrison, London. (reprinted by Leicester University Press in 1971).

R. Bocock, 1986. *Hegemony*. Ellis Horwood, Chichester.

G. Boyd, 1998. 'To Restore the Land to the People and the People to the Land. The emergence of the Not-for-Profit landownership sector in the Highlands and Islands of Scotland'. *Scottish Journal of Community Work and Development* 3, Spring, 1998. (This article is also reprinted in Boyd & Reid, 1999.)

G. Boyd, 1999a. *The Prince, the Merchant and the Citizen. The Need for a Strategic Approach to the Social Land Ownership* Sector. Caledonia Centre for Social Development, Inverness.

G. Boyd, 1999b. *Land Reform and the Failure of Government: Lessons from Scottish Civil Society*. Caledonia Centre for Social Development, Inverness.

G. Boyd & D. Reid, (eds.) 1999. *Social Land Ownership. Eight Case Studies for the Highlands & Islands of Scotland*. Vol.1. Not-for-Profit Landowners Project Group, Inverness.

G. Bruce and F. Rennie, 1991. *The Land Out There: A Scottish Land Anthology*. Mercat Press, Aberdeen.

J. Bryden, 1996. *Land Tenure and Rural Development in Scotland*. The 3rd John McEwen Memorial Lecture, Perth. AK Bell Library, Perth.

A. Calder & A. Gray, 1999. A Leviathan Awakes? p.16. *The Scotsman*, 15 February 1999.

R.F. Callander, 1987. *A Pattern of Landownership in Scotland*. Haughend Publications, Finzean.

R.F. Callander & N. MacKenzie, 1991. *The Management of Wild Red Deer in Scotland*. Rural Forum, Perth.

R.F. Callander, 1995. *Forests and People in Rural Scotland*. A discussion paper prepared for the Forests and People in Rural Areas Initiative. Scottish Office, Edinburgh.

R.F. Callander, 1998. *How Scotland is Owned*. Canongate Books, Edinburgh.

R.F. Callander & A. Wightman, 1998. *Understanding Land*

Reform in Scotland. Proceedings of a conference organised by the Unit for the Study of Government in Scotland (USGS), Edinburgh University, Edinburgh.

E.A. Cameron, 1998. *Scottish Land Reform and the Scottish Parliament*. Paper presented at Symposium on Land and Land Rights, Manchester Metropolitan University, 6 November 1998.

R.H. Campbell, 1991. *Owners and Occupiers: Changes in rural society in south-west Scotland before 1914*. Aberdeen University Press, Aberdeen.

D. Cannadine, 1990. *The Decline and Fall of the British Aristocracy*. Yale University Press, London.

I. Carter, 1975. 'A Socialist Strategy for the Highlands'. In: G. Brown (ed.). *The Red Paper on Scotland*, EUSPB, Edinburgh.

I. Carter, 1979. *Farm Life in North-East Scotland 1840–1914. The Poor Man's Country*. John Donald, Edinburgh.

Centre for Human Ecology, 1996. *Access to the Land. A Case Study Approach to Community Access to the Land Resource*. Centre for Human Ecology, Edinburgh.

G. Corbett & D. Logie, 1997. *Scotland's Rural Housing: At the Heart of Communities*. Report by Shelter and Rural Forum. Shelter Scotland, Edinburgh.

G. Corbett & A. Wightman, 1998. *Housing, Homelessness and Land Reform*. Report by Shelter, Edinburgh.

A. Cramb, 1996. *Who Owns Scotland Now? The Use and Abuse of Private Land*. Mainstream, Edinburgh.

T.M. Devine, 1994. *Clanship to Crofters' War. The Social Transformation of the Scottish Highlands*. Manchester University Press, Manchester.

D. Dewar, 1998. *Land Reform for the 21st Century*. The 5th John McEwen Memorial Lecture, Aviemore. AK Bell Library, Perth.

R.A. Dodgshon, 1981. *Land and Society in Early Scotland*. Clarendon Press, Oxford.

I. Evans & J. Hendry (eds.), 1985. *The Land for the People*. Scottish Socialist Society, Blackford.

S. Foster, A. Macinnes & R. MacInnes (eds.), 1998. *Scottish Power Centres from the Early Middle Ages to the Twentieth Century*. Cruithne Press, Glasgow.

W.M. Gordon, 1989. *Scottish Land Law*. W. Green, Edinburgh.

M. Gronemeyer, 1992. *Helping. In*. W. Sachs (ed.), 1992.

E.P. Harrison, 1995. *Scottish Estate Tweeds*. Johnstons of Elgin, Elgin.

F. Harrison, 1998. *The Losses of Nations. Deadweight Politics versus Public Rent Dividends*. Othila Press, London.

C. Hill, 1991. *The World Turned Upside-Down*. Penguin, London.

E. Hobsbawm, 1962. *The Age of Revolution 1789–1848*. Weidenfeld & Nicolson, London.

J. Hulbert, (ed.), 1986. *Land, Ownership and Use*. Andrew Fletcher Society, Edinburgh.

J. Hunter, 1976. *The Making of the Crofting Community*. John Donald, Edinburgh.

J. Hunter, 1995. *On the Other Side of Sorrow. Nature and People in the Scottish Highlands*. Mainstream, Edinburgh.

J. Hunter, 1991. *The Claim of Crofting*. Mainstream, Edinburgh.

J. Hunter, 1992. Guest Editorial. *Reforesting Scotland* 7, Autumn 1992.

J. Hunter, 1995. *Towards a Land Reform Agenda for a Scots Parliament*. The 2nd John McEwen Memorial Lecture, Dingwall. Rural Forum, Perth.

J. Hunter, 1996. Foreword. In: Wightman, 1996b.

J. Hunter, 1998. 'The Defining Issue: Land Reform and Rural Betterment in the Highlands and Islands'. In: Callander & Wightman, 1998. p. 36.

T. Johnston, 1909. *Our Scots Noble Families*, Forward Publishing Co., Glasgow (reprinted by Argyll Publishing, 1999).

T. Johnston, 1920. *A History of the Working Classes in Scotland*. Forward Publishing Co., Glasgow.

L. Leneman, 1989. *Fit for Heroes? Land Settlement in Scotland After World War 1*. Aberdeen University Press, Aberdeen.

A. Leopold, 1949. *A Sand County Almanac. With Essays on Conservation from Round River*. Oxford University Press Inc., New York.

J. Lister-Kaye, 1994. *Ill Fares the Land. A Sustainable Land Ethic for the Sporting Estates of the Highlands and Islands*. Scottish Natural Heritage Occasional Paper No. 3. Scottish Natural Heritage, Edinburgh.

B. MacGregor, 1993. *Land Tenure in Scotland*. The 1st John McEwen Memorial Lecture, Aberfeldy. Rural Forum, Perth.

D. MacLeod, 1998. 'Land Reform and Human Values'. In: Callander & Wightman, 1998.

K. Marx, 1852. *The Eighteenth Brumaire of Louis Bonaparte*. (Lawrence and Wishart edition, London, 1984).

K. Marx, *Capital*. Lawrence & Wishart, 1976; 1978.

D. Massey & A. Catalano, 1978. *Capital and Land: Landownership by Capital in Great Britain*. Arnold, London.

D. McCrone, 1997. *Land, Democracy and Culture in Scotland*. The 4th John McEwen Memorial Lecture, Perth. AK Bell Library, Perth.

J. McEwen, 1977. *Who Owns Scotland*. EUSPB, Edinburgh.

A. McIntosh, (in press). *The Case for God*. Carbeth Hutters' Feudal Defence against Eviction. Ecotheology.

D. Meek, 1987. 'The Land Question Answered from the Bible: The Land Issue and the Development of a Highland Theology of Liberation'. *Scottish Geographical Magazine*, 10.

W. Ogilvie, 1782. *Birthright in Land*. Reprinted by Othila Press, Teddington, 1997.

W. Orr, 1982. *Deer Forests, Landlords and Crofters*. John Donald, Edinburgh.

Perth and Kinross Fabian Society, 1971. *The Acreocracy of Perthshire*. Perth and Kinross Fabian Society, Blairgowrie.

F. Rennie, 1995. *The Dingwall Agenda*. Ross & Cromarty District Council, Dingwall

J. Robertson, 1998. *Transforming Economic Life. A Millennial Challenge*. Schumacher Briefings 1. Green Books, Totnes.

J.-J. Rousseau, 1754. *Discourse on the Origins of and Bases of Inequality among Men*.

W. Sachs (ed.), 1992. *The Development Dictionary. A Guide to Knowledge as Power*. Witwatersrand University Press, Johannesburg & Zed Books, London; New Jersey.

G. Satterley, 1992. *The Highland Game: Life on Scottish Sporting Estates*. Swan Hill Press, Shrewsbury.

Scottish Executive, 1999. *Land Reform. Proposals for Legislation*. The Stationery Office, Edinburgh.

Scottish Land Commission, 1997. *Public Policy Towards Land in Scotland*. Scottish Land Commission, Edinburgh.

Scottish Law Commission, 1990. *Succession*. Scottish Law Com No. 124. SLC, Edinburgh.

Scottish Law Commission, 1991. *Property Law. Abolition of the Feudal System*. Discussion Paper 93. Scottish Law Commission, Edinburgh.

Scottish Law Commission, 1998. *Real Burdens*. Discussion Paper 106. Scottish Law Commission, Edinburgh.

Scottish Law Commission, 1999. *Report on Abolition of the Feudal System*. Scottish Law Commission, Scot Law Com No. 168. Edinburgh.

Scottish National Party, 1999. *Land Reform in the Scottish Parliament. Scotland's Solutions and Scotland's Opportunities.* Scottish National Party, Edinburgh.

Scottish Office, 1998a. *Identifying the Problems.* Land Reform Policy Group, February 1998.

Scottish Office, 1998b. *Identifying the Solutions.* Land Reform Policy Group, September 1998.

Scottish Office, 1999. *Recommendations for Action.* Land Reform Policy Group, January 1999.

J. Sillars, 1975. 'Land Ownership and Land Nationalisation'. In: G. Brown (ed.). *The Red Paper on Scotland,* EUSPB, Edinburgh.

T. Chris Smout, 1969. *A History of the Scottish People,* 1560–1830. Collins, London.

M. Stiefel and M. Wolfe, 1994. *A Voice for the Excluded. Popular Participation in Development. Utopia or Necessity?* Zed Books, London & New Jersey.

Tilhill Economic Forestry Ltd., 1999. *Forestry of the Future. An Investors Guide to New Woodland Planting on Improved Farmland.* Tilhill, Stirling.

L. Timperley, 1980. 'The Pattern of Landholding in Eighteenth-Century Scotland'. in M.L. Parry & T.R. Slater (eds), *The Making of the Scottish Countryside.* Croom Helm, London.

M. Wigan, 1991. *The Scottish Highland Estate: Preserving an Environment.* Swan Hill Press, Shrewsbury.

A. Wightman, 1996a. *Organisational Profiles: Not-for-Profit Landowning Organisations in the Highlands and Islands of Scotland.* Report prepared for Highlands & Islands Enterprise and Scottish Natural Heritage, Inverness.

A. Wightman, 1996b. *Who Owns Scotland.* Canongate Books, Edinburgh.

A. Wightman, 1998. *The Highland Council Landownership Database.* Highland Council, Inverness.

A. Wightman, 1999. *Land Reform: Politics, Power & the Public Interest.* The Sixth John McEwen Memorial Lecture, Edinburgh International Book Festival, Edinburgh. A.K. Bell Library, Perth.

EXPLANATORY NOTES

Carbeth Hutters a group of tenants occupying holiday huts on
the Carbeth Estate north of Glasgow, some of whom have
been in dispute with their landlord over rent levels. Eviction
notices have been served on a number of them.

Chartist Land Plan a plan by the 19th century Chartist
movement to purchase estates and sub-divide them into
smallholdings.

Citizens' Juries a method of decision making involving lay
citizens hearing evidence and coming to a decision in order to
resolve a dispute or decide on the eligibility of a claim or
proposal.

Commercial Land Company a company formed in 1875
which attempted to raise finance for the purchase of land for
subdivision into smallholdings.

Commonties areas of land owned not by any single owner,
but by the neighbouring landowners collectively. Millions of
acres of such land survived the first five centuries of
feudalism but little is known about how much survives today.
The 9,000 acre Forest of Birse Commonty in Deeside is an
interesting example of a surviving commonty which has
recently been taken over by Birse Community Trust.

Diggers a radical English puritanical group, led by Gerrard
Winstanley, which advocated communal ownership of land in
1649.

Disruption the split in the Church of Scotland in 1843 which
led to the establishment of the Free Church of Scotland. The
split was over the 1712 Patronage Act and the right of
landowners to appoint ministers, a right opposed by those in
the Free Church.

Entail a law introduced in 1685 which allowed a landowner
to predetermine the line of succession to the land and to
shelter it from the claims of creditors. Remaining entails are
due to be abolished as part of the abolition of feudalism.

Farm Woodland Scheme a financial support package to
encourage the transfer of land from agricultural use to forestry.

Feudal the system whereby land is held by a number of different
interests in a hierarchical chain. See Box 1 and Figure 1.

Feuing the process of selling land to another person whilst
retaining an interest in how it is used or developed. This
process makes the seller the feudal superior of the buyer who
in turn is the superior's vassal. See Box 1 and Fig. 1.

Highland Land League a campaigning organisation and
political party founded in 1883 as the Highland Land Law
Reform Association and renamed the Highland Land League
in 1886. It brought together land reformers and scholars
sympathetic to the struggle of the crofting community.

Hypothec the law which allowed a landlord to sequester a
tenant's property in order to recover unpaid rent.

Levellers a group of small tenant farmers and agricultural
workers who protested against landowners' policy of eviction
and clearance in Dumfriesshire and Galloway in 1724.

Mosses wet areas used for the collection of peat fuel.

National Land Company a company set up by the Chartists
through share subscription in 1846 which bought land to be
held co-operatively on behalf of its members.

Patrimonies an inheritance from one's ancestors.

Primogeniture the right of the eldest born male child to
inherit his father's estate.

Register of Sasines the oldest legal register of landed property
in Scotland. It is held by the Registers of Scotland and
contains the deeds affecting virtually all land and buildings in
Scotland and a search of the Register reveals the history of
ownership. This register has, since 1981, been gradually
replaced by the Land Register, a more modern system which
includes computerised mapping of property and a state-
guaranteed title. The Registers of Scotland are at
Meadowbank House, 153 London Road, Edinburgh
EH8 7AU. Tel: 0131 659 6111.

Scottish Land Restoration League a political campaigning
organisation formed in 1884 in Glasgow which called for
radical land reform and the restoration of land to those who
had been cleared from it. John Murdoch, the land reform
campaigner was its first Secretary and stood as its
parliamentary candidate in Partick in the 1885 general
election.

Sporting Rates A levy on the numbers of game killed on farms
and estates. The tax was paid to local authorities until its
abolition in 1995.

Wayleaves rights of access over land provided typically for the
purposes of physical access or the laying of pipes and
erection of transmission lines.

EXTRACTS FROM SOME OTHER LUATH BOOKS

'Increasingly, land is regarded simply as a saleable commodity with no guarantee, under the present laissez faire system, of continuity of stewardship or long term conservation. ... These anomalies may be resolved in the new Land Reform proposals... It is difficult to avoid the conclusion that a far more radical approach is now required to safeguard the public interest over a very large proportion of Scotland's mountain and moorland country.'

Scotland: Land and People – An Inhabited Solitude
James McCarthy
ISBN 0 946487 57 X PBK £7.99

'... the romanticised, trashy version of their own history that the Gael is served up is offered as a sop, a compensation, for the fact that the remaining Gaels live in an area where the land ownership system is an anachronism which symbolises their own expulsion from, and lack of access to, the land of their forebears. Instead of land rights, the Gael has tourist trinket shops. Enthusiasm for some kind of radical land reform in the Highlands is increasing, and our study shows, if anything, that it is not only in the interests of those who live there, but also in the interest of the mountaineers who today visit, that this land reform take place... we can hopefully look forward to the spread of social ownership and the euthanasia of large-scale private landownership over time; and in that time come to accept the view of Marx, that private ownership of landed property is as absurd as the private ownership of human beings.'

Scotland's Mountains before the Mountaineers
Ian Mitchell
ISBN 0 946487 39 1 PBK £9.99

'And still the agricultural land, the once fertile glens and straths, year by year go back to rushes and heather, and the croft houses bear a harvest of Bed and Breakfast signs, and the best crop a crofter can gather is a couple of caravans on the in-bye grazing.
It is time, and more than time, that as much attention be paid to the conservancy of people as the conservancy of nature.'

Luath Guide – The North West Highlands: Roads to the Isles
Tom Atkinson
ISBN 0 946487 54 5 PBK £4.95

'So why is the ownership of sporting estates so important? Are these estates not simply a collection of quaint, irrelevant anachronisms? Rather, from the all-important perspective of rural development, the sporting-estates represent a powerfully negative presence in contemporary Scotland. ... It's as if the ostentatious whims of an essentially foreign (to the Highlands, if not to Scotland as a whole) elite are holding huge chunks of Scotland in suspended animation, governed by the rules and objectives of a neo-Victorian plutocracy... It must, therefore, for most Scots, be galling in the extreme to see so much of this special place locked up in foreign control beyond the financial reach of local individuals or communities or indeed almost anybody but the non-indigenous super-rich.'

Notes from the North
incorporating a Brief History of the Scots and the English
Emma Wood
ISBN 0 946487 46 4 PBK £8.99

'Those were strange days in the Highlands. Enormous estates had been taken over by those newly enriched in the great mid-Victorian burgeoning of industry and trade. They were not interested in the land as a source

of produce or even profit. It was their plaything, a place to be visited for shooting and fishing, and for a few weeks each year, to act out their dreams of lairdship and Highland life... It was not enough to have a vast, empty estate, peopled only by gamekeepers, stalkers and a few shepards. They demanded enormous castles, like Kinloch and the equally preposterous Glenborrodale in nearby Ardnamurchan, in which they played out their dreams.'

Bare Feet and Tackety Boots
Archie Cameron
ISBN 0 946487 17 0 PBK £7.95

'The Government must surely consider some strategic long term plan, in which tourism can play a part, to meet the EEC shortfall and financial support fluctuations in order to assist those who decide to live and work in remote parts of the country...'

Tobermory Teuchter – A First Hand Account of Life on Mull in the Early Years of the 20th Century
Peter Macnab
ISBN 0 946487 41 3 PBK £7.99

'Right at the other end of the social spectrum, though one step up from the labourers by dint of 'possessing' land, were the crofters who inhabited the Highland estates. Untitled and poor, they still lived in houses built from rock and sod, neither read nor wrote, and spoke a 'foreign' tongue...
In that new age of development and improvement they were clearly an anachronism. Not only the landowners, but speculators too, began to see what profits might be wrought from the bleak and unproductive hills of the Highlands.'

Tales of the North Coast
Alan Temperley and the Pupils of Farr Secondary School
ISBN 0 946487 18 9 PBK £8.99

'In these times when so many acres are being taken out of agricultural production for new housing, roads, industrial estates and the like, it is of vital importance that crofting be given its fair chance to make a significant contribution to filling the nation's larder. A school of thought... has advocated the re-introduction of those Government powers... which insisted that land either be used properly or else placed in the hands of someone who would ensure that it was put to good use.'

Crofting Years
Francis Thompson
ISBN 0 946487 06 5 PBK £6.95

'In 1821 there was an expanding, self-supporting population of about 10,000 in Mull and 500 in Iona. By the end of the century those figures were reduced to 4,500 and 150, and were steadily falling.
The destruction of a way of life was done by a new generation of landowners, frequently, although not invariably, newly rich industrialists from England, who had 'bought' the land from the degenerate clan chiefs – although many of them were themselves also directly responsible for horrific clearances.'

Luath Guide - Mull and Iona: Highways and Byways
Peter Macnab
ISBN 0 946487 58 8 PBK £4.95

'Self government or autonomy must mean equal rights and benefits for all citizens or residents in Scotland, regardless of ethnic/national origin.'

old Scotland new Scotland
Jeff Fallow
ISBN 0 946487 40 5 PBK £6.99

Luath Press Limited
committed to publishing well written books worth reading

LUATH PRESS takes its name from Robert Burns, whose little collie Luath (*Gael.*, swift or nimble) tripped up Jean Armour at a wedding and gave him the chance to speak to the woman who was to be his wife and the abiding love of his life. Burns called one of *The Twa Dogs* Luath after Cuchullin's hunting dog in *Ossian's Fingal*. Luath Press grew up in the heart of Burns country, and now resides a few steps up the road from Burns' first lodgings in Edinburgh's Royal Mile.

Luath offers you distinctive writing with a hint of unexpected pleasures.

Most UK bookshops either carry our books in stock or can order them for you. To order direct from us, please send a £sterling cheque, postal order, international money order or your credit card details (number, address of cardholder and expiry date) to us at the address below. Please add post and packing as follows: UK – £1.00 per delivery address; overseas surface mail – £2.50 per delivery address; overseas airmail – £3.50 for the first book to each delivery address, plus £1.00 for each additional book by airmail to the same address. If your order is a gift, we will happily enclose your card or message at no extra charge.

Luath Press Limited
543/2 Castlehill
The Royal Mile
Edinburgh EH1 2ND
Telephone: 0131 225 4326 (24 hours)
Fax: 0131 225 4324
email: gavin.macdougall@luath.co.uk
Website: www.luath.co.uk